The Credit Repair Handbook

Everything You Need to Know to Maintain, Rebuild, and Protect Your Credit

One of the nation's leading bankruptcy attorneys and consumer advocates

JOHN VENTURA

KAPLAN) PUBLISHING

New York

This publication is designed to provide accurate and authoritative information in regard to the subject matter covered. It is sold with the understanding that the publisher is not engaged in rendering legal, accounting, or other professional service. If legal advice or other expert assistance is required, the services of a competent professional should be sought.

Vice President and Publisher: Maureen McMahon
Acquisition Editor: Shannon Berning
Editorial Director: Jennifer Farthing
Development Editor: Sheryl Gordon
Production Editor: Fred Urfer
Typesetter: Maria E. Torres
Cover Designer: Scott Rattray

Published by Kaplan Publishing, a division of Kaplan, Inc.
1 Liberty Plaza, 24th floor
New York, NY 10006

Printed in the United States of America

August 2007
07 08 09   10 9 8 7 6 5 4 3 2 1

ISBN-13: 978-1-4277-5502-5

Contents

Acknowledgments   iv

Introduction   v

CREDIT REPORTING AND CREDIT SCORING

  1. Understanding How Credit Reporting Agencies Affect Our Lives   3
  2. Finding Out What Your Credit Report Says about You   25
  3. Correcting Errors in Your Credit Records   43
  4. What You Need to Know about Your FICO score   61

REBUILDING YOUR CREDIT AFTER SERIOUS MONEY TROUBLES

  5. Credit Rebuilding Preliminaries   73
  6. Going through the Credit Rebuilding Process   93
  7. Getting Credit Rebuilding Help If You Need It   109

AFTER YOU FINALLY HAVE IT: PROTECTING YOUR GOOD CREDIT

  8. Avoiding Financial Problems in the Future   125
  9. Minimizing Damage to Your Credit When You're Having Money Problems   161
 10. The Dangers of Identity Theft   181

Resources   209

Index   215

About the Author   229

Acknowledgments

Thanks to Shannon Berning and Sheryl Gordon who were great to work with and added so much to the book. And a special thanks to my friend and writing partner, Mary Reed. Mary, someone once said you should be grateful to the people who make you happy, they are the gardeners who make your soul blossom. I am grateful for everything you do.

Introduction

As a nationally board certified bankruptcy attorney who has been advising consumers about money matters for nearly 30 years, I have seen first-hand how a bad credit history can affect your life and make it impossible for you to pursue your financial dreams. Some consumers I've counseled had once felt helpless and hopeless because their credit history had made it impossible for them to buy their first home or to purchase a new home to accommodate their growing families. Others had been turned down for better paying jobs because of their bad credit histories or had been denied insurance they needed to help protect themselves and their loved ones. Many of these consumers also found serious errors and misinformation in their credit histories. And, in recent years, a growing number of the consumers I've counseled had credit histories damaged by identity theft.

Regardless of income, education, or age, nearly all of these consumers had one thing in common: they knew little or nothing about credit reporting, credit scores, or their credit reporting rights. Each of the following was also true:

- They were unaware that they had three different credit reports—one with each of the three national credit reporting agencies, Equifax, Experian, and TransUnion—and that the information in each report was a little different.

  Equifax, Experian, TransUnion reports a little different

- They didn't know that they were entitled to obtain a free copy of each of their credit reports, no strings attached, every 12 months by going to a special website set up by the three credit-reporting agencies or by calling a toll-free number.

- They had no idea how to correct inaccurate information in their credit files or how to get outdated information deleted.

■ They didn't know how to rebuild their credit histories after money troubles. In fact, many of them had paid money to credit fix-it firms that had promised to make the negative information in their credit files disappear but had done nothing to help them.

■ They had many misconceptions about credit scoring. For example, they did not realize that most creditors do not use the credit-reporting agencies' own credit scores. Instead, they use consumers' FICO scores (which are discussed in detail in chapter 4); their own proprietary credit scores; or (in the case of some auto lenders) insurance companies, and mortgage lenders, specialized credit scores they purchase. Also, most consumers were unaware that they actually have *three* FICO scores, and didn't know how to raise their FICO scores.

■ They were doing little to protect their personal and financial information from identity thieves, were unaware of their identity theft legal rights, and didn't know what to do when they were victims of that crime.

■ They didn't know very much about personal finance in general, including how to manage their money in order to maintain a good credit history.

For all of these reasons and more, I decided to write an easy-to-understand, comprehensive guide to credit reporting, including information on repairing or rebuilding your credit history after serious money troubles, understanding credit scoring, and avoiding identity theft. This book, *The Credit Repair Handbook,* is the result.

I've divided the book into three parts. The chapters in the first part, "Credit Reporting and Credit Scoring," are essential reading whether your credit history is problem-free or it has been damaged by money problems and/or identity theft. You'll get the lowdown on how credit reporting agencies work, including the kinds of information they collect about you, where they get their information, who uses it, and how they use it to make important decisions about you. You'll learn about the federal laws that regulate the activities of the credit reporting agencies—laws that give you certain rights when you deal with these agencies. You'll find out how to order your credit reports, including when you are entitled to free copies of the reports and how to understand what your credit reports say about you, as well as how to correct any problems you may find. You'll also find out about credit scoring, including the importance of your FICO scores, the factors that go into calculating these scores, and what you can to do to raise your FICO scores.

The chapters in the second part of this book, "Rebuilding Your Credit after Serious Money Troubles," provide consumers who have damaged credit histories with information on how to rebuild those histories. When you read these chapters, you will learn how to use a budget to manage your money and how to build your savings—both are essential not only to rebuilding your credit but to maintaining it. You'll also be encouraged to think long and hard about why your credit histories got damaged in the first place, so that you can avoid repeating any mistakes you may have made that contributed to the damage. Finally, I'll warn you about the dangers of credit repair scams, educate you about the signs of a scam, and offer advice about how to find reliable credit rebuilding help when you need it.

The final part of the book, "After You've Got It: Protecting Your Good Credit," includes chapters with information to help you avoid financial problems in the future. This section features a basic education about money management, credit, and the key federal laws that protect you when you apply for credit, use credit, use your debit or ATM card, pay your bills online, or are contacted by a debt collector. It also explains why it's important to rethink the attitudes about money that may have helped create the problems that damaged your credit, and lays out the various actions you may need to take in order to turn your finances around if they begin to take a turn for the worse, including tightening your financial belt, contacting your creditors, consolidating your debts, and filing for bankruptcy. You'll also learn about identity theft in this part of *The Credit Repair Handbook,* including how identity thieves work, the signs that your identity may have been stolen, and what you should do if you become a victim.

Throughout the book you'll find sample letters, as well as useful forms and sample worksheets. In addition, *The Credit Repair Handbook* features a resource section with books, links, and organizations you can turn to for more information on managing your finances. Use the resource section to find out about other books, as well as magazines, online resources, brochures, and government publications that can help deepen your understanding of the subjects covered in this book.

Now that you understand what you will learn by reading this book, I suggest that you begin with the very first chapter because it introduces you to many of the subjects that I tell you more about in subsequent chapters. It also provides easy-to-understand definitions of many of the words and terms you will encounter throughout this book. So, if you're ready to learn all about credit reporting agencies, credit histories, credit scoring, credit rebuilding, and a lot more, then it's time to turn the page. I wish you lots of luck rebuilding your credit, and years of good credit once you do!

Credit Reporting and Credit Scoring

Understanding How Credit Reporting Agencies Affect Our Lives

1

Credit greases the wheels of life in our society. Sure, you can live on a cash-only basis, but having access to credit with attractive terms makes life easier and makes it possible to purchase big-ticket items that might be beyond your means if you had to pay for them with cash. Among other things, having credit makes it easier to rent a car, make plane and hotel reservations, shop online, take a family vacation at Disney World, help pay for your children's college educations, and buy a home. For all of these reasons, it's essential that your credit histories be full of positive, not negative, information. Also, having positive information in your credit histories makes it easier to obtain adequate insurance, land a good job or promotion, rent a place to live, and so on.

The three national credit reporting agencies (CRAs)—Equifax, Experian, and TransUnion—are quiet giants in your life. You may not be aware of their potential influence, but the credit history information they collect on you and sell to businesses, government agencies, and individuals who are legally entitled to the information can affect your life in profound ways. Most notably, they can make it difficult for you to obtain credit with reasonable terms. It's critical, therefore, that you understand how the CRAs operate—the various kinds of information collected and stored in their computerized databases, who has access to that information, and what they can do with it. You should also be familiar with the federal laws that regulate the CRAs, establish your credit reporting rights, and govern the companies that provide the CRAs with your information. This chapter begins that education by introducing you to the CRAs and to credit reporting in general.

WHAT ARE CREDIT REPORTING AGENCIES?

Credit reporting agencies, also known as credit bureaus, are in the business of collecting and maintaining information on how well you (and nearly every other American consumer) manage your credit accounts. This information, which is a sort of financial report card, is referred to as your *credit history, credit file, credit report,* or *credit record.* The CRAs sell this information to creditors, employers, insurance companies, government agencies, and others who use it to make important decisions about you. Your credit record information is also used to calculate your *credit score,* a three-digit number that predicts how well you're likely to manage your credit in the future. Increasingly, businesses are using this number rather than the actual information in your credit files to make decisions about you and to define the terms of your relationship with them. Chapter 4 gives you more insight into credit scores.

Three corporate giants dominate the consumer credit reporting industry: Equifax, Experian, and TransUnion. Smaller local and regional CRAs are affiliated with one of the "big three." According to the Consumer Data Information Association, the national credit reporting trade organization, the CRAs maintain 200 million consumer credit files, collect 4.5 billion pieces of consumer data every month, and generate one-billion credit reports annually.

THE INFORMATION IN YOUR CREDIT HISTORY

Your credit history includes four basic types of information:

1. **Information about how you've managed your credit accounts over time.** This is the heart of your credit history. For each account listed in this section of your credit report you'll find, among other things, your current account balance, the minimum due each month, whether you've ever been late paying the account, and whether it's ever been sent to a collection agency.

2. **Public record information.** If you've filed for bankruptcy, had a tax lien placed on any of your assets, been arrested or indicted, or have any unpaid money judgments against you (the amount of money that a court ordered you to pay to someone as a result of a lawsuit), that information will show up on this section of your credit history, assuming the information isn't too old to be reported. Information later on in this chapter fills you in on how long various types of negative information can remain in your credit history.

3. **Inquiries.** This section of your credit history lists the creditors, insurance companies, employers, and others who have looked at your credit history information over the past two years.

4. **Identifying information.** Your name and any names you may have used in the past (your maiden name, for example, or your name with a Jr., Sr., II, or III next to it), your current and past addresses, your Social Security number, and the names of your current and former employers are listed in this part of your credit history. Information about your spouse may also appear if you share credit accounts with your spouse, or if your spouse is an authorized user on one of your individual accounts. This means that the account is in your name but you've given him or her permission to use it.

Chapter 2 provides more detail about the various types of information in each section of your credit history.

What's Not in Your Credit History

Your credit history does not contain any information about your religion, race or ethnicity, sexuality, politics, or medical history. (Although a national speciality consumer reporting agency called the Medical Information Bureau (MIB) may be reporting information about your medical history. The last part of this chapter introduces you to the MIB.) You won't find anything in your credit history regarding your checking or savings accounts, your retirement account, or your brokerage account. In addition, don't be surprised if some of your credit accounts are missing from your credit history. The next section of this chapter tells you which ones may not be there.

WHERE THE CRAs GET THEIR INFORMATION

The information in your credit history comes from several different sources. Most of it comes from the creditors who provide the CRAs with regular monthly reports on the status of your accounts. These creditors include banks, savings and loans, credit unions that issue national bank cards (such as Visa and MasterCard) as well as mortgage companies, companies that issue nonbank credit cards (such as American Express and Discover) large national retailers that issue their own store charge cards, and some oil and gas companies, among others.

Some creditors, however, only provide the CRAs with information about your accounts when the accounts are past due or when the creditors have taken an adverse action against you, like turning your account over to collections or writing off one of your accounts as *uncollectible*. These kinds of creditors tend to be medical providers, including doctors and hospitals, utility companies, local retailers, insurance companies, and professionals, such as attorneys and accountants.

If any public record information, such as a bankrupcty, tax lien, or arrest, is in your credit history, it may have come from companies that are in the business of selling information to the CRAs that they find from scouring the records of local, state, and federal courts and government land offices. Also, the CRAs may obtain public record information themselves.

You are also a source of the information in your credit files. For example, when you complete an application for credit and list your name, address, and employment history, that information is apt to end up in the database of at last one of the CRAs.

WHO CAN LOOK AT YOUR CREDIT HISTORY AND WHY

The federal *Fair Credit Reporting Act* (FCRA) is the law that governs the credit reporting industry and establishes your credit reporting rights. Two amendments have been added to that law: the *Consumer Credit Reporting Reform Act* (CCRRA) and the *Fair and Accurate Credit Transactions Act* (FACTA). These acts specify who can look at your credit history information and what they can do with that information. A full copy of the FCRA can be found at *www.ftc.gov/os/statutes/031224fcra.pdf*. The following is a summary of who can see your information and why:

- **Creditors** look at your credit history to help them decide if they will approve your application for new or additional credit. Creditors may also review your credit history to help them decide if they should change the terms of the credit they've already given to you. For example, if the bank that issued you a MasterCard or Visa sees from your credit history that you've frequently been late paying your accounts, it's apt to raise your interest rate, decrease your credit limit, or even cancel the account.

- **Insurance companies** look at your credit history to help them decide if they will sell you insurance, how much insurance to sell to you, and how much to charge for the policy. If you already have insurance, the insurance company may review your credit record information

> **♥ Hot Tip**
>
> Studies show that individuals with good credit histories tend to file fewer insurance claims. Go figure!

when it's deciding whether to increase the cost of your policy or terminate the coverage.

- **Employers** look at your credit history to help them decide if they will hire you, promote you, move you into a different job, or fire you. However, before your current employer or a potential future employer can look at your credit history, it must get your written permission. Also, if an employer decides to take an adverse action against you due in whole or in part because of information in your credit history, the employer is legally obligated to provide you with the name of the CRA it contacted to review your credit history and contact information for that CRA together with a written description of your credit record legal rights. Examples of adverse actions include firing you, not hiring you for the job you may have applied for, and demoting you.

Employers review consumers' credit histories for a number of reasons. They may assume that if a consumer is bad at managing money, he may also be bad at managing other aspects of his life, including work life. Also, some employers worry that someone with serious financial problems may be more tempted to steal on the job, especially if he is responsible for a lot of money. Finally, employers know that money troubles can affect an employee's ability to focus on job responsibilities. For example, money troubles often disrupt marriages, lead people to drink too much or do illegal drugs, cause depression, and make employees more prone to illness.

In addition to or instead of reviewing your credit history, some employers may order an investigative report on you. This kind of report provides a lot of information about your personal life, including subjective information obtained from interviews with people who know you. Investigative reports and your legal rights when an employer wants to order an investigative report on you are discussed later in this chapter.

- **Landlords and rental agents** look at credit histories to help them screen rental applicants. Most landlords don't want to rent to people with a history of late payments or whom a previous landlord has evicted. In addition to the information they obtain from your credit report, some landlords also use residential and tenant reports generated by other national agencies. These other kinds of reports are discussed later in this chapter.

■ **Collection agencies** look at your credit history to help them collect a past-due debt that you may owe. For example, a collection agency may look at your credit history to find out where you live.

■ **Individuals and businesses** with a money judgment against you as a result of a lawsuit might look at your credit history to obtain information that may help them collect on the judgment or decide if they should try to collect.

■ **Potential investors, loan servicers, and current insurers** may look at your credit history to help them assess whether you are likely to live up to a credit obligation you already have with them.

■ **State and local child support enforcement agencies** may look at your credit history to get information about your employment history in order to garnish your wages or to find out where you live.

■ **Other government agencies** may look at your credit history to help determine your eligibility for a license or for government benefits when they are legally required to take into account your financial status. Also, government agencies—the FBI, for example—that are authorized to conduct investigations related to counterterrorism can look at your credit history, if they provide the CRA with the legally required written certification, or if a court orders the release of that information.

■ **Utilities** may look at your credit history to help them decide how large a deposit you may have to pay to obtain new service.

Others who can look at your credit history include the following:

■ Any business or individual that obtains an order from the court granting permission to look at the information. The court order may relate to a lawsuit you initiated or that was filed against you.

■ Anyone that obtains a subpoena as a result of a federal grand jury hearing entitling it to review the information.

- Anyone who has your written permission to look at your credit history.

- Anyone with a "legitimate business need" to review your credit information in connection with a business transaction that you initiated, or to determine whether you continue to meet the terms of an existing account. Some businesses give a broad interpretation to the term *legitimate business need* in order to gain access to your credit record information.

THE IMPACT OF NEGATIVE INFORMATION IN YOUR CREDIT HISTORY

Your credit history will be harmed if it contains negative information, including too many open accounts, high account balances, late payments, defaults, accounts in collection, a bankruptcy, a tax lien because you didn't pay your taxes, and so on. Also, the more negative information there is, the more your finances will be damaged. As a result of the negative information, you may experience the following:

> **❗Hot Tip**
>
> Creditors establish their own individial standards for how much is *too* much negative information in a consumer's credit history. Therefore, some creditors have very high standards and will deny you credit even if you have relatively little negative information in your credit history; others will give you credit even if your credit history contains a lot of negative information, but the credit will come with unattractive terms.

- Being denied the credit you apply for or being approved for credit with less attractive terms, such as a higher than normal interest rate, a lot of expensive fees, and lower credit limits

- Being turned down for a job

- Being denied the life or auto insurance you apply for, being sold less insurance than you applied for, or being charged a higher than normal premium for the insurance

- Having a difficult time finding a landlord who is willing to rent to you

- Being turned down for a government license or security clearance

How Long Negative Information Can Stick Around

The good news about having negative information in your credit history is that it can't stay there forever. The FCRA allows most negative information to be reported for seven years, although some negative information can be reported longer than that. That long-standing information includes the following:

- **Bankruptcies.** All bankruptcies are reported for 10 years. However, the CRAs have a policy of reporting completed Chapter 13 reorganization bankruptcies for seven years.

- **Tax liens.** A tax lien can be reported until you pay it off and then for seven additional years.

- **Civil lawsuits, judgments (the court's official decision in a lawsuit), and arrests.** These will linger in your credit history for seven years after the date that they are recorded with the court.

There are no time limits on the reporting of negative credit record information when you apply for a job that will pay you an annual salary of at least $75,000, for more than $150,000 worth of credit, or for life insurance with a face value of at least $150,000.

YOUR RIGHTS, ACCORDING TO THE FEDERAL CREDIT REPORTING LAWS

Together, the FCRA, the CCRA, and the FACTA establish your rights when it comes to your credit record information and your dealings with the CRAs, as well as with providers and users of that informa-

> ### ✋ Red Alert!
>
> If you're arrested for a crime, the FCRA allows that fact to remain in your credit history for seven years, although some states have laws prohibiting an arrest from being reported unless it results in a conviction or unless you are out of jail and awaiting trial. If you're found guilty of the crime for which you are arrested, there's no limit on how long that fact can be reported. However, the CRAs tend not to report information about arrests and convictions, even though they are entitled to. That information is more likely to show up in a background check that may be run on you (by an employer, for example). To be sure, however, you'll have to order each of your credit histories.
>
> Generally speaking, the older the negative information, the less damage it does to your credit history and the less impact it will have on your life.

tion. They also govern the activities and obligations of the CRAs, information providers, and information users.

The three federal laws give you the right to the following:

- Be notified by creditors, employers, insurance companies, landlords, government agencies, and others whenever they take an adverse action against you due in whole or in part to negative information

> ### ❗ Hot Tip
>
> The FACTA also gives you certain rights when your identity is stolen. Those rights are discussed in chapter 10.

in your credit history. Some examples: if you're denied credit, employment, insurance, or a place to live; the interest rate on the credit you already have is increased; you're demoted; your insurance premium is raised; and so on. You're also entitled to the name, address, and phone number of the CRA that provided the negative information, and to be informed of your right to request a free copy of your credit report from that CRA. However, to qualify for the free report, you must put your request in writing within 60 days of being notified of the adverse action.

- Obtain one free copy of your Equifax, Experian, and TransUnion credit reports every 12 months.

- Obtain additional free copies of your credit history from each of the CRAs if you are unemployed and will be applying for a job within the next 60 days, if you are receiving welfare payments, if a debt collection agency tells you that it has reported (or may report) negative information about you to a credit bureau, or if you are the victim of identity theft.

- Purchase your credit history from any of the CRAs if you are not entitled to a free copy.

- Be notified in writing *before* an employer reviews your credit record information. Also, the employer must get your up-front written permission to look at that information.

- Have a CRA investigate information in your credit report that you believe is incorrect, incomplete (for example, your credit record does not indicate that you paid off a tax lien), or too old to be reported. You are also entitled to have the provider of the information conduct an investigation instead of the CRA. If an investigation confirms that the information you dispute is inaccurate, incomplete, or too old to be reported, you're entitled to have your credit history revised accordingly; e.g., the information may be deleted, changed, or new information may be added to make the original information more complete. If the accuracy of the information you question cannot be verified within 30 days of your investigation request, the information must be deleted from your credit history or changed.

- Ask a CRA that revises your credit history as a result of an investigation to notify any employers who may have looked at your credit history over the past two years of the change and to notify anyone else who looked at it over the past six months. However, you must provide the CRA with the names and addresses of those you want notified, and you may also have to pay the CRA a fee for each notification.

- Have a short statement that you prepare added to your credit history when information that you disputed is not corrected, deleted, or changed in some other way as a result of an investigation. You can use the statement to explain why you believe that the information is inaccurate.

- Receive written, up-front notification whenever an employer or an insurance company orders an investigative report on you, and to learn the nature and the scope of the report if you ask for that information. An investigative report includes subjective information about you gathered from people who know you, like your friends or neighbors. Although creditors are entitled to order investigative reports, they rarely do.

- Be provided the name, address, and phone number of anyone who has looked at your credit history for employment purposes over the past two years, and anyone who has looked at it over the past year for any other reason.

- Purchase your credit score from a CRA for a "fair and reasonable fee," although federal law does not define what that term means.

- File a lawsuit in federal court against a CRA, an information provider, or a user of your credit record information that violates your credit reporting rights. If you win the lawsuit, the court will award you a monetary judgment and you can also collect attorney fees and court costs from the defendant. Depending on the circumstances, you may be able to sue in state court rather than in federal court.

- Limit prescreened or pre-approved offers of credit and insurance. These are the unsolicited offers that you probably find in your mailbox nearly every day. Creditors and insurance companies pay the CRAs to develop lists of consumers to receive these offers based on the information in the consumers' credit files. They are required to include a toll-free number in their offers that you can use to opt out of receiving additional offers in the future.

🖐 Red Alert!

Trying to exercise your rights with the CRAs can be frustrating sometimes. Resolving even the simplest issue can become complicated and can trap you in a maze of letters, emails and toll-free numbers that always bring you right back where you started—with an unresolved question or problem.

What to Do If You Think Your Rights Have Been Violated

You can take a number of different actions if you believe that a CRA, a provider of information to a CRA, or a user of that information has violated your federal credit record rights. Those actions include sending a complaint letter to whomever you believe committed the violation, filing a complaint with the Federal Trade Commission (FTC), and filing a lawsuit. A consumer law attorney who has specific experience resolving violations of the federal credit reporting laws can help you determine your best course of action. For a referral to a consumer law attorney in your area who can help you, contact the National Association of Consumer Advocates at (202) 452-1989 or at *www.naca.net* or the National Consumer Law Center at (617) 542-8010 or at *www.consumerlaw.org*.

Reporting a Violation to the FTC

When you believe that your credit reporting rights have been violated, contact the FTC. Although it won't take action on your behalf alone, it is important to let the FTC know what has happened to you. If it receives enough complaints about a specific CRA, information provider, information user, or business practice, it may take legal action to protect consumers in general.

You can contact the FTC in writing at: Federal Trade Commission, Consumer Response Center, 240, 600 Pennsylvania Avenue, N.W., Washington, DC 20508. You can also call the FTC at 1-877-382-4357, or file your complaint online at *www.ftc.gov/ftc/consumer.htm*.

🤚 **Red Alert!**

Never try to handle your own lawsuit when your federal credit record rights have been violated. Your chances of winning your lawsuit will be slim to none because such lawsuits tend to be complicated, and because the defendant will be represented by an attorney.

FILING A LAWSUIT

If your case is strong, the attorney will probably represent you on a *contingent fee basis,* which means that you won't have to pay the attorney any money up front. Instead, if the attorney wins the lawsuit, she will take the fee out of the money that the court awards you. If the attorney loses, she won't be compensated for the time and effort. Win or lose, however, you'll probably be expected to reimburse her for any expenses incurred handling your case. Be sure that all of the terms of your agreement with a consumer law attorney are spelled out in writing.

Your lawsuit may allege that the defendant was either of the following:

- **Willfully noncompliant.** This means that you believe the defendant knowingly violated the law. When you bring this type of lawsuit you can sue for actual damages, which is the money you spent as a result of the defendant's illegal actions, such as attorney fees and court costs, and any wages you may have lost because you had to take time off from work without pay to deal with your legal problem. You can also sue for emotional pain and suffering if the defendant's behavior had an extremely negative impact on your life (you had to be treated for depression, for example), as well as for punitive damages. Courts award punitive damages in order to help discourage defendants from repeating their illegal behavior.

- **Negligently noncompliant.** This means that you were harmed by the CRA, information provider, or information user, and you don't allege that the harm was intentional. When you bring this kind of lawsuit, you can only sue for actual damages plus attorney fees and court costs.

You can also sue anyone who obtains a copy of your credit report under false pretenses or who knowingly obtains a copy without a legally permissible purpose. For example, a creditor may claim that it will use your credit record information to determine whether to give you new credit, but in fact, it uses the information for some other purpose. Another example: someone who's not entitled to access your credit history (an identity thief perhaps) uses your information. Under such circumstances, you can sue for actual damages or for $1,000 (whichever is less), your attorney fees, and punitive damages. It's also possible that the defendant will be prosecuted criminally. If convicted, the defendant could be required to spend up to two years in prison and pay a fine.

OTHER NATIONAL CONSUMER REPORTING AGENCIES THAT ARE GOVERNED BY THE FCRA

The CRAs are just one of many different types of *national consumer reporting agencies.* These other agencies also collect information on you, such as information about your medical records, your residential or tenant history, your check-writing history, your history filing insurance claims, or your personal background. They sell your information to employers, insurance companies, and landlords.

These other types of agencies are also governed by the FCRA and are required to comply with all of the same provisions that apply to the CRAs. For example, they must correct an error in your file if an investigation that you initiate confirms the error, and they are obligated to provide you with a free copy of your file every 12 months, assuming you request it. However, because there's no central, comprehensive list of all of these other national consumer reporting agencies, it's not easy to know who these agencies are and how to contact them. As a result, you may not find out that one of those agencies has information about you until you're denied employment, insurance, a place to rent, or something else because of the information. Also, ordering a free annual copy of the information can be a challenge because federal law doesn't require these other agencies to maintain a centralized website or a single, central 1 800 number for ordering copies of your reports from them. However, federal law *does* require each of them to establish a toll-free report ordering number.

The following provides general information about the larger national consumer reporting agencies and tells you how to order a free annual copy of the information they may be reporting about you:

The Medical Information Bureau (MIB). The MIB collects and maintains medical-related information on consumers with significant medical conditions like epilepsy, asthma, diabetes, and so on, who have applied for individual life, health, long-term care, or disability insurance. The MIB's information is available to insurance companies that may be thinking about selling insurance to these consumers, but the consumers must give their up-front written permission first. Most consumers do not have an MIB file. In fact, according to the MIB, only about 20 percent of all consumers have one. To find out if you're one of those consumers—and if you are, what's in your file—go to *www.mib.com/html/request_your_record.html*. You can also call 1-866-692-6901.

Check-reporting companies or registries. These kinds of agencies report information on your check writing, including how often your checking account is overdrawn, how often you write bad checks, and whether a bank, savings and loan, or credit union has ever closed your checking account. If one of these companies has a lot of negative information on you, you may have a hard time finding a financial institution willing to give you a checking account.

The businesses on the following list represent the major check-reporting companies. The list provides information for contacting each to find out if they have information on you and to obtain a free copy of that information:

- **Certegy.** Go to *www.certegy.com/ContactUs* and click on "Consumer Assistance" at the top of the page, or call 1-866-543-6315.

- **CheckRite.** Call 1-800-766-2748.

- **ChexSystems.** Go to *www.consumerdebit.com/consumerinfo/us/en/index* or call 1-800-428-9623.

- **Shared Check Authorization Network (SCAN).** Go to Chex-Systems' website or call 1-800-262-7771.

- **TeleCheck.** Call 1-800-835-3243.

Businesses that collect and sell information to insurance companies about the automobile and/or homeowners' insurance claims you may have filed in the past. Insurance companies use this information to help them assess the likelihood that you will file insurance claims in the future. The information can affect your ability to obtain adequate insurance, as well as the cost of your insurance.

The two largest national insurance speciality reporting agencies are Choice Point and ISO Insurance Services. Choice Point produces auto claim and insurance claim CLUE Reports. To order your free annual CLUE Reports, *go to www.choicetrust.com* or call 1-866-312-8076. To obtain your free annual A-Plus Report from ISO, go to *www.iso.com/products/*, or call 1-800-627-3487.

Companies that report on your rental history. When you apply for a place to rent, the landlord or rental agent may order your history from one of these companies to find out if you paid your rent on time in the past, left your previous apartments in good condition when you moved out, and so on. If too many blemishes appear in your rental history, your application may be turned down.

Most companies that provide rental history information do not classify themselves as *national* consumer reporting agencies. Therefore, because the federal credit reporting laws do not apply to them, they're not obligated to provide you with a free annual copy of the information they are reporting about you. However, three rental history reporting firms do operate as national companies. Their names and the information you need to order your free annual reports follow:

- **ChoicePoint.** Go to *www.choicepoint.com* or call 1-877-448-5732.

- **SafeRent.** Call 1-888-333-2413.

- **Tenant Data Services.** Call 1-800-228-1837.

Background screening companies. These companies provide consumer background check reports to employers. An employer may order such a report about you when you apply for a job. Also, your currrent employer may order one when you apply for a promotion. Insurance companies sometimes order background check reports as well. Background check reports can include a wide range of information, including your credit record information, information about your education, your work history, state licenses, driving record, medical history, whether you ever filed a workers compensation claim, whether you have a criminal record or have been incarcerated, the results of any drug testing you may have submitted to, and basic information about your military history, such as your rank, duty assignments, salary, recognitions, and your current status in the military.

✋ Red Alert!

The FCRA applies to most background check reports. However, the law doesn't apply when a background check is run on you because you're being considered for a job with an annual salary of at least $75,000. Also, the law doesn't apply when an employer conducts its own background check rather than hiring an outside company to do it. Now that so much information is available on the Internet through free and for-a-fee databases, many employers do their own employee background checks.

Given the sensitive nature of the information in background check reports, an employer cannot order one on you without first obtaining your written permission. (The same restriction applies to insurance companies.) The employer must provide you with a special form to sign that is separate from any job application you are asked to fill out and from any other job-related paperwork you may be given. Also, if the employer wants the report to include your medical records, your high school and/or college transcripts, financial aid records, and/or information about any disciplinary actions your school may have taken against you, the employer must ask you to sign additional consent forms. The FCRA does not obligate the employer to tell you ahead of time which company will run your background check.

If an employer decides not to hire you because of information in your background check report (or if it decides to take some other adverse employment-related action against you), it must provide you with notice of its decision prior to making it official, together with a copy of the report it reviewed, and information about your rights under the FCRA. Once the employer takes the adverse action, it must notify you of that fact and provide you with the name of the background screening company, as well as its address and phone number, and inform you of your right to dispute any information in your background screening report that you believe is inaccurate or incomplete.

Investigative reports. These are background check reports that also include subjective information about your character and reputation, lifestyle, and personal habits—information obtained through interviews with your friends, neighbors, and family members. If an employer wants to order an investigative report on you, it must get your up-front permission using a special form that's different from the one it must use when it orders a regular background check. In addition, you are entitled to ask the employer to explain the nature and scope of the investigation before giving your permission. All

> **❗ Hot Tip**
>
> If there is negative information in your background report, some employers will let you explain the information and will give you a certain number of days to try to clear up the infomation if you believe it is inaccurate or incomplete.

🖐 Red Alert!

When an employer orders a background check report about you from a background screening company, the FCRA entitles you to a free annual copy of the report. However, most of those companies don't collect and maintain information about consumers like the CRAs do. Instead, they collect information on an as-needed basis—whenever they are asked to prepare a background report. In fact, at the time that this book was written, only ChoicePoint collects and maintains consumer background check information. To find out if ChoicePoint has a file on you, and to order a free annual copy of your file if it does, go to *www.choicepoint.com* or call 1-866-312-8075.

of the same FCRA requirements that apply to regular background check reports also apply to investigative reports, and you also have the same rights under the FCRA vis à vis an investigative report as you have in regards to a regular background check.

The next chapter will deepen your understanding of the national credit reporting agencies and credit reporting in general by explaining how to order copies of your Equifax, Experian, and TransUnion credit reports, and how to understand what your reports say about you. You'll learn how to order your reports through the mail, by phone, and online, as well as how to find out when you are entitled to free copies of your credit reports, and about the various kinds of information in each report.

🖐 Red Alert!

Besides all of the national consumer reporting agencies that may be collecting and reporting information about you, other specialty agencies that are not national may be doing the same thing. However, because they aren't national, they're not covered by the FCRA. Also, some agencies that are national avoid having to comply with the law by operating in such a way that they don't qualify as a national consumer reporting agency. However, some states have passed laws to regulate them. Contact your state attorney general's office to find out if your state is one of them.

Terms to Remember

This chapter used a number of words and terms that may be new to you. You will encounter many of them as you read other chapters in this book. This short glossary defines each of those words and terms.

Adverse action—A harmful action that a business or government agency takes against you as a result of negative information in your credit histories. The action may include: turning you down for credit, denying you the job or promotion you applied for, demoting you, rejecting your application for insurance, refusing to rent to you, increasing the cost of the credit you already have, charging you more for your existing insurance premium, and so on.

Background check report—A report that contains much more detailed information than a consumer credit report. In addition to including your credit record information, a background check report may also provide details about your educational and work histories, your driving record, your medical history, any workman's compensation claims you may have filed, and your criminal record (if you have one), among other things. The FCRA requires anyone who orders a background check report to comply with special rules.

Contingent fee basis—The way that some attorneys charge for their services. When a consumer law attorney charges on a contingent fee basis, he or she does not charge you an up-front fee for representing you. Instead, if you win, the losing side—the defendant—pays your attorney for the number of hours he or she spent on your case as part of the judgment. If you lose your case however, your attorney does not get paid for his or her time.

Credit history (also referred to as a credit file, credit record or credit report)—Detailed information about how a consumer has managed his or her credit acccounts over time. A credit history also includes identifying information about a consumer such as the consumer's Social Security number and current address, negative public information about the consumer, like information about a tax lien, an arrest or an incarceration, as well as the names of the businesses who reviewed the consumer's credit record information.

Credit score—A three-digit number based on the information in a consumer's credit history signifying how well or how poorly the consumer has managed his or her credit accounts.

Default—When a consumer doesn't live up to the terms of his or her agreement with a creditor in regards to a credit card account, a loan, or a line of credit.

Equifax—One of the three national credit reporting agencies that collect, maintain and sell information about consumers' credit accounts.

Experian—One of the three national credit reporting agencies that collect, maintain and sell information about consumers' credit accounts.

Terms to Remember continues on next page

Terms to Remember continued from previous page

Fair Credit Reporting Act (FCRA)—The federal law that governs the credit reporting industry and that gives consumers specific protections and rights in regard to their credit histories, the national credit reporting agencies, and other types of national specialty consumer reporting agencies. Since the FCRA was passed, Congress has amended the law two times, with passage of the Consumer Credit Reporting Reform Act (CCRRA), and the Fair and Accurate Credit Transactions Act (FACTA).

Federal Trade Commission—The federal office charged with enforcing the FCRA and other consumer protection laws.

Investigative report—A type of consumer report that includes subjective information about a consumer that has been acquired from the consumer's friends, neighbors, relatives, and others who know the consumer. Consumer credit reports do not include subjective information.

Legal judgment—The official decision of the court in a lawsuit. For example, the court may order the defendant to pay the consumer a certain amount of money. This is called a *money judgment.*

National consumer speciality reporting agencies—An umbrella term that applies to all types of national businesses that collect and sell consumer information to employers, insurance companies, and landlords and that are governed by the FCRA. In addition to consumer credit record information, these agencies may collect and sell information about consumers' medical records, rental histories, insurance claims or personal background, among other kinds of information.

National credit reporting agency (also called a credit bureau)—A type of national consumer specialty reporting agency that collects information about how consumers manage their credit accounts over time, maintains that information in computerized databases, and sells that information to whomever is entitled to see it according to the FCRA. The national credit reporting agencies are Equifax, Experian and TransUnion.

Prescreened or pre-approved offers—Unsolicited offers of credit or insurance. The FCRA allows consumers to opt out of receiving such offers.

Tax lien—A legal claim on a consumer's real or personal property by a taxing authority, like the IRS, as a result of the consumer's failure to pay her taxes. The consumer cannot sell, borrow against, or transfer the property with the lien attached to it without paying the taxing authority first. The lien also gives the taxing authority the right to take the property from the consumer in payment for her tax debt.

TransUnion—One of the three national credit reporting agencies that collect, maintain and sell information about consumers' credit accounts.

Finding Out What Your Credit Report Says About You

2

Now that you've read chapter 1 and understand the importance of the information in your credit history, it's time to order a copy of your Equifax, Experian, and TransUnion credit histories so you can find out what they say about you. This chapter tells you how to do that, including how to order the reports for free once a year, and how to order them for a fee if you need to.

This chapter also reviews the basic types of information you'll find in your credit reports and explains why the details of that information will probably differ a little from report to report. Last but not least is a discussion of some of the other credit report–related products that the credit reporting agencies (CRAs) market to consumers, and whether it's worth paying for any of those other products.

REVIEW ALL THREE OF YOUR CREDIT HISTORIES, NOT JUST ONE

When you are ready to find out what's in your credit history, don't order the information from just one of the CRAs; order it from all three. Here's why:

- The CRAs don't get their information from exactly the same sources. For example, one creditor may report information about your account to Experian; another may report your account information to Equifax and TransUnion; and a third may report to all three CRAs.

- There may be a serious problem in one of your credit histories that doesn't appear in your other two. The problem may be misinformation, outdated information, or incomplete information. Furthermore, when you apply for credit, employment, insurance and so on, you probably won't know which of your credit histories will be reviewed during the application evaluation process. Therefore, it's important to make sure that all of your credit files are problem free.

It's a good idea to review each of your credit histories every six months because new information is constantly being added. You should also review them a couple months before you apply for important credit, employment, insurance, and so on, so that you'll have time to address any problems before you file your application. Chapter 3 explains how to resolve credit record problems.

OBTAINING YOUR CREDIT HISTORIES FOR FREE

Although the Fair Credit Reporting Act (FCRA) says that the CRAs can charge you a reasonable fee for each copy of your credit history that you order, you're entitled to free copies of your credit reports under certain circumstances. For example, the Fair and Accurate Credit Transactions Act (FACTA) gives you the right to obtain a free annual copy of each of your credit reports. It also gives you the right to obtain free copies of your credit reports when you know or believe that you're the victim of identity theft.

The next two sections of this chapter tell you how to order your free annual credit reports, and about the specific special circumstances that entitle you to additional free copies. Chapter 10 discusses obtaining free copies when your identity has been stolen.

How to Order Your Free Annual Credit Reports

Every 12 months, you can order one free copy of your Equifax, Experian, and TransUnion credit reports. You can order them all at the same time or you can order them individually throughout a 12-month period. Your free reports should arrive about 15 days after you place your order.

There are three ways to order your free annual reports:

1. Order them online at *www.annualcreditreport.com*. This is the report-ordering website that the three CRAs were required to establish under federal law.

2. Order by phone at 1-877-322-8228.

3. Order by mail. You can write a letter requesting one or more of your free annual credit reports or you can download a request form at *www.annualcreditreport.com/cra/requestformfinal.pdf*. Fill it out completely and mail it to: Annual Credit Report Request Service, PO Box 105281, Atlanta, GA 30348-5281.

🤚 Red Alert!

AnnualCreditReport.com is the *only* website that offers you all three of your credit reports for free, no strings attached. Other sites, like FreeCreditReport.com, may claim to offer free credit reports, but all of their offers come with a catch—you're automatically signed up to receive a "free" service, such as credit monitoring for a limited time, for example. Once that time is up, your credit card is automatically billed each month for the cost of the service, unless you remember to cancel the service.

If you write a letter, your request won't be processed unless the letter contains very specific information. To make sure that you include all of the required information, model your letter after the sample in Figure 2.1. Also be sure to indicate in your letter whether you are ordering all three of your free annual credit reports, or just one or two. If you are ordering one or two, be clear about which one(s) you want. Send your letter or your request form via certified mail with a return receipt requested so that you will know when your request is received.

🖐 Red Alert!

Some identity thieves set up websites offering free credit reports, but the sites are nothing more than a means of obtaining your personal and financial information. Watch out, because some of these sites have URLs that at first glance appear to be the official free annual credit report website established by the CRAs. If you get scammed by a phony site, file a complaint with the FTC at *www.ftc. gov,* visit its identity theft Web site at *www. consumer.gov/idtheft,* and follow the advice in chapter 10. Also, if you receive a suspicious email about your credit reports or come across a credit report–related website that you don't think is legit, contact the Los Angeles Electronic Crimes Task Force run by the Secret Service at *LA.ECTF.reports@usss.dhs.gov* and *spam@uce.gov.*

When you order one or more of your free annual credit reports via a letter, be sure that it contains all of the information in this sample letter. Your order can't be processed without it:

FIGURE 2.1 Sample Letter for Ordering One or More of Your Free Annual Credit Reports

[Date]
Annual Credit Report Request Service
PO Box 105281
Atlanta, GA 30348-5281

To Whom It May Concern:
I am writing to request a copy of my free annual credit report from ___ _____ [*indicate which CRA credit report(s) you are ordering*]. The following information is provided to help you process this request:

* [*Your full name, including Sr., Jr., III, etc.*]
* [*Your Social Security number. To help protect you from identity theft, you can request that when the CRA processes your order, it not print the last five numbers of your Social Security number on your credit report.*]
* [*Your date of birth*]
* [*Your spouse's full name, if you are married*]
* [*Your spouse's Social Security number*]
* [*Your current address, and your previous address(es) if you've not lived at your present address for at least two years. Include your apartment number or private mailbox number if appropriate.*]
* [*Your evening and daytime phone numbers, including area codes*]

Please mail my credit report(s) to: [*Provide your name and mailing address*].
Thank you in advance for your prompt attention to this request.

Sincerely,
[*Your signature*]

OTHER TIMES THAT YOU'RE ENTITLED TO FREE COPIES OF YOUR CREDIT REPORTS

The FCRA also entitles you to free copies of your credit histories, in addition to your free annual copies, when either of the following happens:

- A creditor, employer, or insurance company takes an adverse action against you (such as lowering your credit limit, canceling your account, or increasing the cost of your policy), in whole or in part because of negative information in one of your credit histories. The company taking the adverse action must provide you with the name and contact information of the specific CRA that reported the negative information so you can contact it to request a free copy of your credit report. However, you must make your request within 60 days of receiving the company's notice or you'll have to pay for the report.

> **▼ Hot Tip**
>
> When you order your credit report online, you can revisit the report for 30 days regardless of whether you order a free report or pay for it. After 30 days, you will have to pay to review your credit report again. When you place your online order, you will be asked to establish an ID and password. Save the ID and password because you won't be able to return to your online credit report during the 30-day period (or file a dispute online) without them.
> If you don't, retrieving your ID and establishing a new password can be a time consuming and frustrating hassle.

- You add a fraud alert to your credit files because you think or know for sure that you are the victim of identity theft. Chapter 10 focuses on identity theft.

You are also entitled to a free report from each of the CRAs within any 12-month period (in addition to your free annual credit reports) if any of the following applies:

- You are out of work, but intend to apply for a job within the next 60 days. When you make your request, provide written certification of your current job situation and your intention to apply for a new job within the required time frame. Attaching a copy of your last unemployment check to your certification—or some other document that helps prove your unemployment—will help expedite your request.

- You're receiving public welfare assistance. You must certify in writing that you are receiving public assistance. Attaching a copy of your most recent public assistance check to the certification helps ensure that your request will be processed in a timely manner.

- A collection agency lets you know that it has reported or is about to report negative information about one of your credit accounts to a CRA. You are only entitled to a free credit report from that particular CRA.

If any of these circumstances apply to you, you must contact the CRAs individually to order copies of your credit histories. Contact information for each of the CRAs appears later in this chapter.

In addition to what federal law says about getting free copies of your credit reports, your state may have a law that also entitles you to one or more free credit reports for any reason every 12 months. These free credit reports are in addition to the federally mandated free annual credit reports.

At the time this book was written, Colorado, Georgia (which entitles residents to two free copies of credit reports every year), Maine, Maryland, Massachusetts, New Jersey, and Vermont all had such laws. If your state isn't on this list, check with your attorney general's office to find out if your state has passed such a law since this book was written.

PAYING FOR YOUR CREDIT REPORTS

If you have already obtained your free annual credit reports in a given 12-month period and you don't qualify for additional free reports for any reason, you'll have to pay a fee each time you order a copy of your credit report from a CRA. The cost of a credit report was $10 at the time this book was written. (You may also have to pay a sales tax, depending on your state.) Some states have laws that permit their residents to purchase copies of their credit reports for less than $10. To find out if your state is one of them, call your state attorney general's office.

ORDERING YOUR CREDIT REPORTS FROM EACH OF THE CRAS

You can order additional copies of your credit histories from Equifax, Experian, and TransUnion online at their websites, by phone, or by mail. Figure 2.2 provides detailed ordering information for each of the CRAs.

> **❗ Hot Tip**
>
> To help protect your Social Security number from identity thieves, when you order your credit reports by mail, ask each of the CRAs not to print the last five digits of that number on your credit reports.

Ordering your credit histories online is your fastest option, because once you've completed the ordering process and paid for your report using a major credit card, you'll get immediate access to your credit record information. You can also print a copy of your online credit report. In contrast, ordering by mail is the slowest way to obtain copies of your credit records. Refer to the sample letter in Figure 2.3 to make certain that your letter includes all of the requisite information.

> **🤚 Red Alert!**
>
> Selling credit report–based products and services to consumers is a big business for the CRAs. When you visit their websites, the first thing you'll see are bundles of products and services that the CRAs want you to buy rather than purchasing just a single copy of your credit report. As a result, if you are ordering your credit report online, it can be a challenge to figure out where to go on the site to place your order. However, the online ordering information included in Figure 2.2 makes it easy for you to navigate these sites.

FIGURE 2.2 Ordering Additional Copies of Your Credit Reports After You've Ordered Your Free Annual Reports

Follow these instructions to order your credit report from one of the CRAs when you've already ordered your free annual report.

- **Equifax**
  - To order online, go to *www.equifax.com*. At the top of the page, use the pull-down menu under "Products" to select "Equifax Credit Report," which will bring you to the order page. Word to the wise—to make certain that you are billed for your Equifax credit report *only* and not for any other Equifax products or services, click on the circle at the right of the page next to the words "Get only your Equifax Credit Report for $10.00," and unclick the box on the right-hand side of the page next to the words "Add Equifax Credit Ranking for only $8.95."
  - To order by phone, call 1-800-685-1111.
  - To order by mail, send your request to Equifax Information Services, LLC Disclosure Department, PO Box 740241, Atlanta, GA 30374-0241.
- **Experian**
  - To order online, go to *www.experian.com/consumer_online_products/index.html* and click on the yellow "Order Now" button at the bottom of the column labeled "Experian credit report."
  - To order by phone, call 1-888-397-3742.
  - To order by mail, write to Experian, National Consumers Assistance Center, PO Box 2104, Allen, Texas 75013-2104.
- **TransUnion**
  - To order online, go to *www.transunion.com* and then click on "FACT ACT" at bottom of your screen under the heading "More for Consumers." At the bottom of that page you'll see a highlighted area to click on to order a single copy of your TransUnion credit report.
  - To order by phone, call 1-800-916-8800.
  - To order by mail, mail your request letter to TransUnion, Consumer Disclosure Center, PO Box 2000, Chester, PA 19022-2000.

If you decide to order a copy of your credit report from a CRA through the mail, it's essential that you include specific information in your letter. Otherwise, the CRA won't be able to fill your order until you provide the missing information, which means that there will be a delay in processing your order. Model your letter after this one to make certain you include all of the vital information:

FIGURE 2.3 Sample Letter for Ordering Your Credit Report by Mail When You Have to Pay

[Date]
[Name of CRA]
[Address of CRA]

Please send me a copy of my credit report. The following information is provided to help you process this request:

* [Your full name, including Sr., Jr., III, etc.]
* [Your Social Security number]
* [Your date of birth]
* [Your spouse's full name, if you are married]
* [Your spouse's Social Security number]
* [Your current address, and your previous address(es) if you've not lived at your present address for at least two years. Include your apartment number or private mailbox number if appropriate.]
* [Your evening and daytime phone numbers, including area codes]

I have enclosed a _____ [check or money order] in the amount of $10.00 to pay for my credit report. [Depending on your circumstances or state, you may not need to include the previous sentence, or the amount of your check or money order may be a different amount.]

Please mail my credit report to: [Provide your name and mailing address].

Thank you in advance for your prompt attention to this request.

Sincerely,
[Your signature]

OVERVIEW OF THE INFORMATION IN YOUR CREDIT REPORTS

Although the format of and the specific information in each of your credit reports will vary from CRA to CRA, as you learned in chapter 1, all three reports include the same four basic types of information:

1. Identifying information. In this part of your credit history, you'll find your personal information, including your name and any other names you may have used in the recent past, your current and past addresses, your Social Security number, date of birth, and the names of your current and past employers. Depending on which CRA generated the report, your phone number, spouse's first name, and the type of residence you live in (e.g., single or multifamily home) may also be included.

2. Account information. This is the heart of your credit history because it's where you'll find information about your individual and joint credit accounts (accounts you share with someone else—your spouse or partner, probably). Among other information, for each of the accounts listed in this section you'll find the following:

- Account number (the number may be scrambled to help protect you against identity theft.)

- When you opened the account and when the credit reporting agency began reporting information about the account

- Type of account—whether it's a revolving or installment account, a mortgage, or some other type of loan

---

🖐 **Red Alert!**

Having a lot of credit-related inquiries in your credit history is not a good idea because creditors may interpret them as an indication that you are taking on more debt than you can handle.

- Whether the account is an individual or joint account

- If the account has been closed; if it has been, your credit report should indicate whether you closed it or whether the creditor closed it because of your poor payment history

- The account's outstanding balance at the time the credit report was generated

- The monthly amount due for installment accounts, mortgages, and other kinds of bank loans that require you to pay a set amount each month.

- The account's current payment status: on time, paying as agreed, or late, for example; also, the number of days you may be late paying the account: 30 days, 60 days, 120 days, and so on

- The original amount of a loan and your total credit limit for other types of accounts

- The most you've ever owed on the account

- If the account has been turned over to collections

- If the account has been written off or charged off as uncollectible

3. Inquiries. This section of your credit reports indicates who (including you) has looked at your credit history information, and when. Each time someone requests your information it's referred to as an *inquiry*. Anyone who looks at your credit history will see some types of inquiries, but only you will see all of them. All credit-related inquiries, for example, are seen by everyone and are referred to as *voluntary* or *hard* inquiries. However, only you will see employment-related inquiries, inquiries made by your existing creditors in order to monitor the state of your finances, inquiries that are the result of your reviewing your own credit history, and inquiries that appear because you subscribe to a credit monitoring service. This service, which is offered by each of the CRAs, alerts you whenever information is added to your credit history that may be a sign of identity theft.

Inquiries that are the result of a preapproved offer of credit or insurance, or "promotional" inquiries, are also seen by you only. A preapproved offer is a firm offer that you did not solicit. Usually it states that you've been approved for a credit card or insurance, and that all you have to do to take advantage of the offer is fill out and return the enclosed form or call a certain phone number. Preapproved offers happen when a creditor or an insurance company asks a CRA to review the information in its database in order to develop a list of consumers to whom the business will send its offer.

4. Public records information.
This section of your credit report presents information about you that may be in court records. The following are some examples of the kind of information you may find:

> ▼ **Hot Tip**
>
> You can opt out of receiving preapproved offers for five years by calling 1-888-567-8688, the toll-free opt-out number established by the CRAs.

- The IRS or your state taxing authority has a lien on one of your assets because you didn't pay your income or property taxes. As long as there's a lien on the asset, you can't borrow against it or sell it unless you pay what you owe.

- There are unpaid court judgments against you. For example, one of your creditors sued you for nonpayment of a debt that you owe and, as a result, the court has ordered you to pay a certain amount of money to the creditor. That amount is called a *money judgment*.

- A business or individual has put a judgment lien on one of your assets in an effort to collect money that you owe. Until you get the lien removed by paying what you owe, you can't borrow against the asset or sell it.

- Your mortgage lender foreclosed on your home or some other piece of real estate that you owned.

- Your car was repossessed.

- You were arrested for a crime.

- You failed to comply with the terms of a court order requiring you to pay child support.

HOW THE CRAs ORGANIZE THE INFORMATION IN YOUR CREDIT HISTORY

When you receive your Equifax, Experian, and TransUnion credit reports, you may find them confusing at first, given the amount of information they contain, the slightly different reporting formats each CRA uses, and the abbreviations that the CRAs use to present information. However, all of the reports contain the same basic types of information. After you spend time reading them, they will begin to seem less daunting.

You can see a preview of what each CRA's credit report looks like if you order it online:

- **Equifax.** Go to *www.equifax.com*. Click on "Equifax Credit Report" using the pull down menu under "Products," which is toward the top left of the page. Next click on the words "sample credit report" under the words "See it in ACTION."

🖐 Red Alert!

If you receive your credit reports via regular mail, they may look a little different than the sample reports you'll find online. However, your online and your mailed credit reports contain the same information.

- **Experian.** Go to *www.experian.com*. Click on "View all products" at the bottom of the page. On the "product overview" page click on "Experian credit report" and then on "View sample report" at the far right side of the page.

- **TransUnion.** Go to *www.transunion.com.* Click on "TrueCredit Learning Center" at the bottom right of the opening page. Then click on "How to read your credit report" under the heading "RELATED ITEMS" at the far right side of the page.

OTHER PRODUCTS SOLD BY THE CRAs

If you visit the CRAs' websites, you'll immediately notice that each is peddling a bewildering array of products and services related to your credit report and your credit score. They also market products and services via pop-up ads. For example, in addition to selling single copies of your credit report, they sell the following:

- Three-in-one credit reports

- Three-in-one credit reports with a credit monitoring service

- Three-in-one credit scores

- Credit score monitoring

- Three-in-one credit score monitoring

- A single copy of your credit report with credit monitoring

- A single copy of your credit report and the credit score derived from that report with credit monitoring

The list goes on and on and on. Furthermore, if you purchase just a single copy of your credit report and nothing else, before you complete your order the CRA may encourage you to upgrade your order by trying to sell you additional products and services. Also, if you call a CRA's customer service the CRA representative you speak with may deliver a sales pitch before ending your call.

A lot of what the CRAs want you to buy is a waste of money. For example, a three-in-one credit report, which can cost you as much as $34.95, is a good example of a product that's probably not worth purchasing. This kind of report is often advertised as something that will make it easier for you to compare the information in your credit histories. However, comparing the three reports on your own isn't all that difficult, assuming you're willing to spend a little of your own time and effort. Also, it's a waste of money to buy a three-in-one report if you haven't yet ordered the three credit reports you are legally entitled to every 12 months, or if you're entitled to free copies of your credit reports for some reason.

In addition, it usually doesn't make sense to purchase a service that monitors your credit scores, because most creditors, insurance companies, and so on will check your FICO scores (not the CRA's scores) when they are making a decision about you. However, if you are about to rebuild your credit history, there's an argument to be made for using a three-in-one credit score monitoring service from a CRA as a means of measuring the impact of your rebuilding efforts. For example, if your scores are rising, you can assume that you're doing a good job of rebuilding your credit. Once you have rebuilt your credit history, however, the service won't be worth a lot to you.

One service that you may want to consider, however, is credit monitoring. This service keeps track of the information added to your credit history and notifies you whenever anything unusual or suspicious is added that could be a sign of identity theft. There is value in getting an early warning about possible identity theft—if you have been victimized, the sooner you learn what has happened and take steps to deal with the theft, the less damage the thief can do to your finances and to your credit history. Chapter 10 discusses identity theft in depth, including how to avoid becoming a victim and what to do if it happens to you.

If you decide to purchase a credit monitoring service, you'll also have to decide whether you want to pay for three-in-one credit monitoring, or whether you want to pay each CRA to monitor just the information it has on you. It's a toss up as to which is best. According to some critics of three-in-one monitoring, the CRA from whom you purchase the service may monitor the information in its own database on a regular basis (weekly or daily) but monitor the information in your other two credit files just occasionally. This undermines the rationale for subscribing to three-in-one-credit monitoring in the first place and argues for ordering a separate credit monitoring service from each of the CRAs. However, subscribing to three different credit monitoring services gets expensive, considering that, when this book was written, the three subscriptions would cost you a total of nearly $350 annually. In contrast, the cost of a three-in-one credit monitoring ranged $59 to $180 per year, depending on from which CRA you bought the service.

Some critics scoff at credit monitoring services entirely. They argue that you can monitor your own credit reports by ordering and reviewing them periodically. However, these critics assume that you will remember to order the reports regularly and that you will actually take the time to carefully review each of them. If you're like many people, your intentions may be good, but you may never get around to taking either step.

When you review your three credit histories, you may find that they contain inaccurate, out-of-date, or incomplete information. The FCRA gives you the right to dispute that kind of information with the CRA that is reporting it or with the creditor that provided the information to the CRA. The next chapter reviews the most common kinds of credit record problems, explains why you should correct any problems you may find in your credit histories, and guides you through the dispute process.

Correcting Errors in Your Credit Records

3

Numerous national studies have shown that it's not at all uncommon for consumers to find errors in their credit files, including inaccurate information, incomplete information, or information that is too old to be reported. The errors may be the result of mistakes made by the credit reporting agencies (CRAs) or by the creditors that provide consumer account information to the CRAs, or they may be the result of identity theft.

Regardless of what caused them, errors in your credit files can be costly. For example, you may be charged a higher interest rate on credit than you would if your credit files were error-free (or even be turned down for credit); be denied a job, a professional license, or a security clearance; be charged more for your insurance; or be rejected for insurance. Also, among other negative consequences, the errors in your credit files may lower your credit scores.

🖐 Red Alert!

Being charged a higher rate of interest on a loan or credit card because of problems in your credit history can cost you hundreds, if not thousands, of extra dollars, depending on the account's outstanding balance and the interest rate.

If you find an error in one of your credit files, the Fair Credit Reporting Act (FCRA) gives you the right to initiate an investigation into the problem with the CRA that is reporting the error, or with the creditor that may have provided the CRA with the erroneous information. You also have the right to have that information corrected if the investigation confirms the error. The law also establishes a general investigation process and time line. Unfortunately, however, getting wrong credit record information corrected can sometimes be easier said than done. In fact, some consumers have spent months and even years trying to resolve serious errors in their credit histories.

This chapter arms you with the information you need to make the investigation process work for you. It alerts you to the most common types of credit record errors so that you'll know what to look for when you review your credit histories, guides you through the error investigation process, warns you about potential shortcomings and stumbling blocks in the process, and offers advice for handling them. Reading this chapter is no guarantee that the investigation process will work smoothly for you if and when you find an error in your credit history, but it can help increase the likelihood that you'll get the error corrected eventually.

REVIEW ALL THREE OF YOUR CREDIT RECORDS FOR ERRORS

The best way to avoid paying a price for errors in your credit histories is to order a copy of your three credit records every six months. Review their information line-by-line for accuracy and completeness, and dispute any errors you may find. Also, whenever possible, you should review your credit histories a few months before you apply for something important, so that you'll have time to resolve any credit record errors before you file your application.

It's important for several reasons to review all three of your credit records and not just one or two. As you learned in the previous chapter, the information in each of those records may vary somewhat, so there may be errors in one of your credit files that don't appear in your other two. Also, when you apply for credit, rental housing, insurance, and so on, you probably won't know ahead of time which of your three credit histories will be looked at during the application review process, or which of your credit scores will be checked out. Therefore, it's essential that you keep tabs on all of your credit record information and correct all problems as soon as you discover them.

✋ Red Alert!

You cannot get rid of negative but accurate credit record information using the investiga-tion process. Only time can make that kind of information go away.

COMMON ERRORS YOU MIGHT ENCOUNTER

The following list summarizes the kinds of errors that consumers most often find in their credit files. Be alert for them when you review your Equifax, Experian, and Trans Union credit histories:

- There are errors in your identifying information. Your name is misspelled, your Social Security number is wrong, your street address is incorrect, you are listed as a "Jr." when you are a "Sr.," and so on.

- Account information is incorrect. For example, your credit report shows that you paid an account late when you've always paid the account on time, has the wrong account balance, has the wrong account number, and so on.

- Accounts that you closed are being reported as open. Be sure that your credit report indicates that *you*, not the creditors, closed the accounts. Otherwise, it will appear as though the accounts were closed because you didn't keep up with your payments.

🖐 **Red Alert!**

Having too many open accounts will harm your credit history and lower your FICO scores. However, don't close any accounts you no longer use, because by doing so, you are apt to do additional damage to your FICO scores. Instead, don't use the accounts and try not to open any new accounts.

- Someone else's account information is in your credit history. This is most likely to happen if you and someone else share the same or similar names.

- Debts that your spouse acquired prior to your marriage are in your credit history. Those debts should not appear in your credit file because they are your spouse's individual debts, so you have no responsibility to pay them.

- Negative information that is too old to be reported is still in your credit record. Most negative information can be reported for seven years, although some types of information can be reported for longer. Chapter 1 explains how long various types of negative information can remain in your credit files.

- Accounts that were turned over to a collection agency are listed twice—under the name of the original creditor *and* under the name of the collection agency.

- Information is incomplete. Your credit history doesn't tell the whole story about something in your credit file. For example, it doesn't reflect the fact that you paid off your mortgage.

AN OVERVIEW OF THE INVESTIGATION PROCESS

If you find an error in one of your credit histories, you are entitled to ask the CRA that reported the information or the information provider—which will usually be a creditor—to conduct an investigation into the error. If the investigation confirms the error, you can ask to have your credit record corrected. Correcting the information may involve deleting it, changing it, or adding additional information to make your credit history more complete.

If the investigation concludes that your credit file contains no error, the information you disputed will stay there. Also, the information provider will continue to share the negative information with the CRAs that it works with.

✋ Red Alert!

A CRA or an information provider can refuse to investigate an error if it believes that your request for an investigation is frivolous or irrelevant—i.e., you've provided no real basis for one. You must be notified of this fact in writing within five days of your investigation request, and you must be given a written reason for the refusal, as well as an explanation of what additional information you would have to provide in order to trigger an investigation. However, it will be a very general explanation, so it won't be especially helpful to you.

INITIATING AN INVESTIGATION WITH A CRA

Most consumers who discover an error in one of their credit histories initiate an investigation with the CRA that produced the report. You can do that in the following ways.

Use the CRA's dispute form. If you order your credit report by phone or through the mail, it will either come with a dispute request form that you can complete and return to the CRA, or with information telling you how to obtain the form. Most likely, you will be told to go to the CRA's website to print a form that you can mail back to the CRA, or to use the CRA's online dispute form. Access each of the CRAs' online dispute forms in the following ways:

- **Equifax.** Go to *www.equifax.com.* Click on the words "Online Dispute" at top of page.

🖐 Red Alerts!

- If you order your credit report online, you will be asked to choose a password and an ID number. Hold on to that information because you will need it if you want to view your report again during the 30 days following your order, or if you want to file an investigation request online. If you don't keep that information, retrieving your ID from the CRA and getting a new password can sometimes be problematic.

- Although using the CRA's dispute form makes it easy to initiate an investigation, it has some drawbacks. One drawback is that you must describe the error in your credit file by choosing from a series of possible errors that are printed on the form, none of which may adequately explain your particular problem. Also, the forms tend to provide you with only a very small amount of space to provide an additional explanation. Finally, if you file your dispute online, you can't provide the CRA any documentation you may have that help corroborate the error you want investigated at that point in time. So if the errors listed on a CRA's online dispute form don't do a good job of describing the problem you are disputing, and/or if you have backup information that you want the CRA to review when it considers your dispute, initiate your dispute by sending the CRA a letter.

- **Experian.** Go to *www.experian.com.* Click on "Disputes" at bottom of page.

- **TransUnion.** Go to *www.transunion.com.* Click on "Dispute an item on your report" at bottom of page.

Use a typed letter. In your letter, clearly and concisely explain the error in your credit file. Avoid generalities such as "I disagree with the information you are reporting about my XYZ credit account," because you won't provide the CRA with enough information to help you. Explain specifically why you believe the information is incorrect or incomplete, and indicate exactly what you want the CRA to do about it. For example, say "I have a zero balance on my credit card account with XYZ company (Account #XXXXX). However, your records show that my outstanding balance is $1,000. Please correct your records to reflect the zero balance. I have attached a copy of my most recent account statement from XYZ company, which reflects the zero balance." Include your name, address, and daytime phone number. Also, if the front page of your credit report includes a confirmation number (it may also be referred to as an account or file number), include that number in your letter, too. Figure 3.1 provides a sample letter you can use as a model. Mail your letter to the CRA's address for disputes, which will be indicated either on your credit report or on the dispute form that came with your credit report.

Model your letter after this one to ensure that you provide the CRA with all of the information it needs to investigate an error in your credit history. Make a copy of the letter for your files, and send the letter to the CRA using certified mail with a return receipt requested:

FIGURE 3.1 Sample Investigation Request Letter

[*Date*]
[*Your name*]
[*Your address*]
[*Your Social Security number*]
[*Credit report confirmation number*]

Dispute Department
[*Name of CRA*]
[*Address of CRA*]

To Whom It May Concern:

I am writing to dispute the following items in my credit report:

[*List each item you are disputing, including the name of the creditor and the account number as applicable. Clearly explain why the information is wrong. For example, the account; does not belong to you; the full amount of this debt was discharged in bankruptcy on a certain date; you have never been late with this account, and so on. Also, next to each error, explain what you want done. For example, you want the account that doesn't belong to you deleted from your credit history; you want your credit history to show a zero balance for the debt that was discharged in bankruptcy; or you want the account that you have always paid on time to reflect that fact.*]

I have attached copies of the following documents in support of my dispute.
[*List exactly what you are enclosing*]

Also attached is a copy of my credit history with the error(s) I am disputing highlighted. If you have any questions, I can be reached at [*Your daytime area code and phone number*].

Sincerely,
[*Your signature—sign your name as it appears on your credit history*]

Enclosures: [*List each document you are attaching to your letter*]

❗Hot Tips

Try to keep your letter to one page. If your letter is longer than one page, the information on the other pages may never get read. Also, do not hand-write your letter because your writing may not be clear.

■ Whenever you initiate an investigation by writing a letter or by printing the CRA's dispute form and mailing it in, attach to your request a copy of the page from your credit history where the error appears and use a highlighter to circle the error. Also, make a copy of your form or letter before you send it to the CRA, and send it via certified mail with a return receipt requested so you know when your investigation request was received, and the date by which the CRA is obligated to respond to you.

■ When you initiate an investigation with a CRA, send a copy of your dispute form or letter to the provider of the information you are disputing. Even though the CRA is supposed to share your information with the provider, it's a good idea to be doubly sure that the provider has everything it needs to help confirm an error.

A key benefit of writing a letter is that you have plenty of space to describe the error in your credit history and to explain what you want done about it. Also, you can attach to your letter copies of any documents you may have that help corroborate the error you want corrected. Those documents may include correspondence, receipts, cancelled checks, court records, account statements, and so on.

Call the CRA's toll-free dispute line. The number to call should be indicated on your credit report or on the dispute information that should come with the report. Although initiating an investigation by phone is faster than using the mail, it has some disadvantages. First you'll have no written record of your dispute. You may regret not creating a paper trail if you encounter problems getting the error cleared up. Second, you have no guarantee that the information you provide about the error in your credit history will be recorded accurately, regardless of whether a CRA employee or a computer takes down what you say. Third, using the phone makes it impossible to provide the CRA with information that helps corroborate the error in your credit file at the same time that you initiate the investigation. Although you can send the information later, you have no guarantee that whoever is involved in the investigation will see it.

What Happens Next

Within five business days of receiving your investigation request, the CRA must ask the provider of the information that you are disputing to confirm the accuracy of the information. The CRA must forward on to the provider all relevant data related to your dispute, including any backup documentation you provided. In turn, the information provider must review all of the information, as well as its own records, to determine whether there is an error in your credit file, and it must report its conclusion to the CRA.

> **! Hot Tips**
>
> - If the first page of your credit report includes a confirmation number, account number or file number, be prepared to provide that number when you initiate an investigation by phone.
>
> - The FCRA entitles you to request an expedited investigation from a CRA if you are applying for a home mortgage or a car loan.

If the information provider confirms the error, it must correct the information about your account that's in its database, and it cannot report the wrong information to the CRAs again. Also, if the information provider does not verify the accuracy of the information you've disputed within the 30-day investigation period, the FCRA requires it to revise your account information according to what you requested when you initiated your dispute. For example, let's assume that one of the CRAs is reporting that you've paid a particular account late and you know that you've always paid it on time, so you dispute that information with the CRA and ask that the payment history for that account be revised accordingly. If the creditor associated with the account doesn't get back to the CRA within the legally required deadline to confirm or deny the accuracy of the information you've disputed, the FCRA requires the creditor to remove the late payment information from its database, even if you are wrong and you have been late with some of your account payments. Also, the CRA can no longer report that you've been late with the payments. However, if the information provider later provides the CRA with proof that in fact you did pay the account late, then the information you disputed can be put back into your credit file.

YOUR RIGHTS IF AN ERROR IS CORRECTED

When an information provider confirms an error to the CRA, the CRA must correct your credit record information. For example, depending on the exact nature of the error, it may do the following:

- Correct inaccurate information in your credit file

- Make your credit file more complete by adding information

- Delete outdated information

- Remove information from your credit file that doesn't belong to you

The CRA must also notify the other two CRAs about the correction so that they can correct their own databases as necessary. In other words, if you found the same error in more than one of your credit files, you only need to dispute the error with one of the CRAs.

In addition, the CRA must provide you with a free copy of your corrected credit report together with the following:

- A statement of the results of the investigation.

- A notice of your right to have a copy of your corrected credit report sent to any employers who may have reviewed your credit history over the past two years, and to anyone else who may have looked at it over the past six months. However, you'll have to provide the CRA with the names and addresses of whomever you want to receive a copy. The CRA is entitled to charge you a fee for each report it sends out at your request.

- A notice that you can request a description of the process used to investigate the error in your credit history, together with the name and contact information of the information provider.

The CRA must provide you with this information within five business days of completing its investigation. It must complete the investigation within 30 business days of the date that it receives your investigation request (45 days if you provide the CRA with additional information during those 30 days). *If it fails to do so, it must correct your credit history as per your request even if the information you disputed is accurate.*

AFTER THE ERROR IS CORRECTED

A month or two after an error in your credit history is corrected, order another copy of that record to make sure that the erroneous information hasn't reappeared. Although the CRAs are supposed to have systems in place to prevent errors from being reinserted, it still happens sometimes. If the error is back in your credit history, gather the notice you received from the CRA telling you that the error had been corrected, along with the copy of your corrected credit report that it sent you, and then call the CRA. If the CRA corrects your credit record again, ask for written confirmation and another copy of your credit report. A month or two later, confirm that the error hasn't reappeared.

If the error you corrected also appeared in one or both of your other credit histories, order copies of them as well so you can make sure that the error has not also reappeared there. If it has, write a letter to whichever CRA is reporting the erroneous information to ask it to correct your credit file, and attach to the letter a copy of the initial notice you received from the CRA that conducted the investigation informing you that the error had been resolved.

🖐 Red Alert!

When information in your credit file is changed as a result of a CRA's investigation, but the provider of the information later certifies to the CRA that the information you disputed was in fact complete and accurate, the CRA is entitled to undo whatever change(s) it made to your credit file. It must notify you of what it has done within five business days, and must provide you with the name, address, and phone number of the information provider.

IF THE INVESTIGATION DOESN'T CORRECT THE ERROR

If the CRA's investigation concludes that your credit file contains no error, then the information you disputed will remain in your credit history and will continue to be reported. However if you are sure you are correct in your dispute, don't give up! Here are some other steps you can take to try to resolve your problem:

- Find additional information to help prove the error, and send a copy of this information to the CRA, together with a letter that references the outcome of its investigation and asks that your credit history be corrected in light of the new information you are providing.

- Prepare a written statement of up to 100 words explaining why you believe that the information in your credit history is in error and send it to the CRA that conducted the investigation. It must make the statement a part of your credit history so that anyone who reviews it can read the statement. However, the value of written statements is diminishing now that a growing number of creditors, insurance companies, and other groups are using credit scores to help them make decisions about consumers rather than reviewing actual credit histories. One way to deal with this fact is to attach to your application a copy of your credit history with the statement highlighted and to try to discuss the details of the statement with the applicable decision maker.

- File a complaint against the CRA and/or against the information provider with the FTC. The FTC won't help you clear up the error, but if it receives a lot of complaints like yours, it may take legal action against the CRA and/or the information provider.

- Consult with a consumer law attorney. Depending on the particulars of your situation, you may have grounds for a lawsuit against the CRA, the information provider, or both.

- Contact the provider of the erroneous information to discuss the error you want corrected. You may be able to resolve your problem by phone, although it's more likely that the information provider will ask you to send it a letter describing the error that you want corrected and to attach to your letter any information that helps corroborate the problem. Contacting the information provider is an important step, because the CRA may not have forwarded to it all of the information you shared with the CRA when you initiated the investigation. Or, if the CRA did forward everything, the information provider may not have reviewed carefully all of your information. Ask the information provider to send you a written notice of its conclusion. If it confirms the error, the information provider must correct its database immediately, notify all of the CRAs that it works with about the correction so they can revise their own databases, and notify you in writing about what it has done.

❗ Hot Tip

If the information provider confirms the error in your credit history, make copies of the notice you receive informing you of that fact. Send a copy of this notice to each of the CRAs that is reporting the error, together with a letter demanding that they correct your credit records accordingly. Although the information provider is legally responsible for notifying them, communicating directly with the CRAs yourself provides you with extra insurance that your credit files will be corrected. When it comes to resolving problems in your credit records, it pays to cross every *t* and dot every *i*.

INITIATING AN INVESTIGATION DIRECTLY WITH AN INFORMATION PROVIDER

With the passage of the *Fair and Accurate Credit Transactions Act*, you are now entitled to initiate an investigation into an error in your credit file directly with the provider of the erroneous information, rather than working through the CRA that is reporting the information. If you go this route, contact the information provider to find out how to initiate an investigation, because the process will vary. What doesn't vary, however, is the information provider's legal obligation to investigate, to report its conclusion to you within the same time frame that applies to investigations conducted through a CRA, and to provide you with the same written notices. If the information provider confirms an error, it must correct its own database immediately, and immediately report the correction to all of the CRAs with whom it shared the incorrect information so they can correct their databases, too. While an information provider is conducting its investigation, it cannot report the information you are disputing without indicating that it is "in dispute."

If the information provider's investigation fails to correct the error, you can take any of the next steps that are available to you when a CRA's investigation does not resolve an error, including adding a written statement to your credit file(s).

WORDS TO THE WISE ABOUT INVESTIGATIONS

Although federal law spells out a process for correcting problems in your credit histories, don't assume that the process will go smoothly or that you'll achieve the outcome you want right away. Based on the experiences of many other consumers with problems in their credit histories, you should be prepared to be frustrated—resolving credit record problems can take months of back and forth communications with a CRA and/or with an information provider. Every bit of persistence and patience you have may be tested. In fact, some consumers end up having to hire consumer law attorneys to help them resolve their credit record problems.

Investigations can be problematic for a number of reasons, including the following:

- If you use the CRA's dispute form, the options you have for describing what's wrong with your credit history may be too generic to accurately convey the error in your credit history.

- If you provide the CRA with backup documentation to help prove an error, the CRA may not review it or may not forward the documentation to the information provider. If it is forwarded, the information provider may not read the documentation thoroughly.

- The information provider may do a poor job of analyzing its own data.

- The employees of the CRA and/or information provider handling your investigation may not be well trained.

For all of these reasons, it's a good idea to maintain detailed records about an investigation from the very start. Not only will this information help you track the progress of an investigation, it can also be very helpful if the investigation doesn't resolve your problem. In fact, if you have to go to court to get your credit history corrected, your attorney may use the information in your records to help build your case.

Your records should include the credit report containing the error you want corrected, a copy of the dispute form you completed or the letter you wrote, the date that you called the CRA or the creditor if you initiated your investigation by phone, originals of any backup documents you may provide to the CRA and/or to the information provider, all correspondence or notices you receive related to the investigation, and copies of any letters you write in response. Also, maintain a record of any phone conversations you have with the CRA and/or the information provider, including the date of each conversation, the name and title of whomever you speak with, a summary of the conversation, and the details of any promises that are made to you.

The next chapter tells you all about credit scores, the three-digit numbers derived from your credit record information. The chapter focuses most of its attention on your FICO credit scores, which are the specific kind of score that most creditors use. After reading the chapter, you'll understand the various factors that go into calculating your FICO scores and how to raise them.

✋ Red Alert!

Always try to write down the details of your phone conversations immediately after you hang up the phone, when they are still fresh in your mind. If you wait even a day, you may forget something important about the conversation or some of the facts may be a little fuzzy.

What You Need to Know About Your FICO Score

4

Do you know your credit score? The three-digit number, which is derived from your credit record information and calculated using a mathematical formula, is a measure of how well you've managed your credit in the past and how well you're likely to manage it in the future. A growing number of creditors, insurance companies, employers, and landlords consider your credit score when they make decisions about you. Although it's probably not the only factor they will take into account, your credit score can pack a powerful punch.

This chapter explains how credit scoring works, tells you about the various types of credit scores, and zeros in on the Classic FICO score—the "big daddy" of all credit scores and the one that really counts. The chapter also explains how to order your FICO scores, reviews the factors that can cause your scores to sink or soar, and offers tips for raising them.

WHO'S KEEPING SCORE?

You don't have just one credit score; you have many scores, all calculated using different formulas. For example, each of the three credit reporting agencies (CRAs) has its own credit scoring formula and sells consumer credit scores based on those formulas on their websites. Also, some large mortgage lenders and insurance companies have developed their own customized credit scores for making decisions about consumers (these credit scores are not available to consumers), and the Fair Isaac Corporation calculates a variety of different credit scores, including the FICO score.

Each of your credit scores changes constantly as information is added to or deleted from your credit files. So if your credit scores are low right now because you mismanaged your credit or experienced a financial setback like a job loss or a serious and costly illness, they will rise as your finances start to improve and as you begin repairing your credit histories, assuming that all of the information that you add to them during the rebuilding process is positive.

THE CRAs' CREDIT SCORES

You can purchase a credit score from each CRA by going to its website. Your CRA credit scores will vary from CRA to CRA because each uses a different formula to calculate consumer credit scores, and because the information in your credit file varies from CRA to CRA. Another reason for the differences in your CRA credit scores is that each of them uses a different numerical range to rank your credit score. For example, Experian credit scores range from 330 to 830; Equifax credit scores fall somewhere between 300 and 850; and TransUnion scores range between 150 and 934.

Your Experian and TransUnion credit scores are *estimated* or *educational* scores. In other words, although they are a measure of your credit risk, they're not as predictive of your future behavior as are your FICO scores. Therefore, although they are sold to consumers, most creditors, insurance companies, and others looking for information about you do not make decisions based on either of these credit scores. However, your Equifax credit score is actually a FICO score. That means it's not an estimated score, which means that creditors, insurance companies,

and others who just want to check out that score and not all three of
your FICO scores may order it directly from Equifax.

The three CRAs have collaborated on the development of another
type of credit score called the *VantageScore,* which is calculated using
information from all of their files. It differs from other types of credit
scores in that it ranks you with a number between 501 and 990, as well
as with a letter between A and F. Although the CRAs developed the
VantageScore to compete directly with the FICO score, to date it's not
widely used. In fact, at the time this book was written, only Experian
was selling it, at *www.vantagescore.experian.com.*

FOCUSING ON YOUR FICO SCORES

Your FICO score is the score to zero in on because it's the one used
by most creditors. According to information available at *www.myfico.
com,* a website of Fair Isaac Corporation (the company that created
and sells the score), 90 percent of all large banks and most mortgage
lenders use the FICO score. In fact, it's such a popular decision-
making tool that the terms *FICO score* and *credit score* have become
virtually synonymous.

Fair Isaac produces a number of different credit scores, but the specific
type of score most important to you
is your *Classic* FICO score, because
it's the one at which most creditors
look. You actually have three Classic
FICO scores (one based on the information in each of your credit files),
each of which ranges from 300 to 850.

> **❗ Hot Tip**
>
> When you apply for new or additional
> credit, many creditors—mortgage lend-
> ers especially—look at all three of your
> Classic FICO scores and then use the
> one in the middle.

Although the standard for an acceptable FICO score varies by user,
generally speaking you're considered a very good credit risk if your
score is 700 or more, which means that you'll be offered more attractive terms of credit and lower premiums than consumers with lower
scores. If your FICO score is at least 650, most creditors and insurance
companies will do business with you, but if your score is lower than

that, you're apt to have problems getting credit with reasonable terms and affordable insurance, and you'll be less attractive to employers and landlords. Your FICO score isn't the only criteria that those decision makers will take into account, however, when they evaluate you. For an overview of other criteria that creditors may take into account, see chapter 8.

Fair Isaac also calculates two other types of credit scores—the *NextGen* and the *Expansion* scores. These are specialized scores with mathematical formulas that are different from the one used to determine your Classic scores. The company developed the Expansion score to help creditors make decisions about consumers who have little or no credit histories, whereas many auto lenders use the NextGen score. Fair Isaac does not sell either type of score to consumers.

FINDING OUT YOUR FICO SCORES

You can buy your FICO Classic scores individually for $15.95 (each score comes with the credit report from which it is derived) or you can purchase all three scores and credit histories at one time for $47.85. To make a purchase, go to *www.myfico.com* and click on "Shop." Then scroll down to "FICO Deluxe" to buy all three scores and reports, or to "FICO Standard" to buy just one score. After you pay for your purchase using a major credit card, you'll get instant online access to your score(s) and report(s).

> **❗ Hot Tip**
>
> You can purchase your Equifax Classic FICO score from Equifax. It's the only one of the CRAs that sells a FICO score.

When you purchase one or more of your FICO scores, you'll also receive an explanation of the various factors, both positive and negative, that affected your score(s), access to the *FICO Score Simulator*—which you can use to calculate how your score(s) will be affected if you pay off a debt, open a new account, and so on—and tips for what you can do to increase the scores. If you have questions about your Classic FICO scores or the Score Simulator, call 1-800-319-4433, the customer support number for myFICO.com.

It's a good idea to order all three of your three FICO scores every six months and review them along with your credit histories. Do the same a couple months before you apply for important credit, insurance, employment, and so on, so that you will have time to clear up any problems in your credit files that might be lowering your credit scores. The "Tips for Raising Your FICO Scores" section of this chapter also provides advice about how to increase them.

🖐 Red Alert!

A sudden drop in one of your FICO scores may be a sign that your identity has been stolen, if the thief's use of your personal and financial information added a lot of negative information to the credit history on which the score was based.

THE FACTORS THAT DETERMINE YOUR CLASSIC FICO SCORES

Your Classic FICO scores are based on five factors, each of which is given a different weight or importance in Fair Isaac's scoring formula. The following are the five factors, from most important to least important:

1. **Your account payment history (35 percent of each credit score).** Your scores will suffer if your credit histories show that you've paid creditors late or exceeded your credit limits on some of your accounts. Information showing that you've had accounts turned over to collections, filed for bankruptcy, or had a tax lien put on an asset that you own, is especially harmful to your credit scores.

2. **The total amount that you owe to your creditors and the total amount of credit that you have access to; i.e., your total credit limit.** (30 percent of each credit score). Owing a lot to your creditors, having high credit balances relative to your total credit limits (balances that amount to more than 35 percent of your total credit limits are generally considered too high) and having a lot of open credit accounts lowers your FICO scores.

> **▼ Hot Tip**
>
> Generally, new credit record information is more important than older information. Therefore, if your financial problems are behind you and now you are paying your debts on time, those problems won't harm your FICO scores as much as if you are still struggling financially.

3. **How long you've had a credit history** (15 percent of each credit score). You get "extra points" if you've had credit for many years and if you've had credit with many of the same creditors for a long time. The longevity makes you appear financially stable and responsible.

> **🖐 Red Alert!**
>
> If you have a lot of open credit accounts, your FICO scores will be harmed even if the accounts have low or zero outstanding balances. This is because as long as they are open accounts, you could run up the balances and begin having trouble paying your creditors as a result. However, if you have a lot of open accounts, don't close them. Closing accounts can harm your credit scores, too. Remember, a better approach is not to use the accounts and not to open up any new accounts unless absolutely necessary.

4. **The amount of credit you've applied for recently** (10 percent of each credit score). Generally, even one recent application for new credit will lower your credit scores a little. However, after a month or two, your credit score should begin to improve, assuming you manage the new credit well and everything else in your credit history stays the same.

5. **Your credit mix** (10 percent of each credit score). Having a mix of different types of credit, such as a Visa or MasterCard, a mortgage, and car loan, can boost your FICO scores. The assumption is that if you can manage the mix well, you are a better credit manager than consumers who don't have a similar variety of types of credit. However, don't try to

> **▼ Hot Tip**
>
> Fair Isaac's scoring formula won't penalize you if you shop for a mortgage or a car loan within a concentrated time—within the same 14-day period—because no matter how many applications for a mortgage or car loan you may submit during that period, the formula treats them as single inquires.

improve your scores by applying for a lot of different types of credit, because all those credit applications will have the opposite effect. You're better off instead raising your FICO scores by following the advice in the next section.

TIPS FOR RAISING YOUR FICO SCORES

If your Classic FICO scores are in the pits, don't despair. You can do some things to raise them, such as the following:

- Regularly review each of your credit files for errors, incomplete information, and outdated information, all of which can lower your credit scores. If you find any of these problems, get them corrected as quickly as possible by following the instructions in chapter 3.

- Stay alert for signs that your identity has been stolen. If an identity thief opens new credit accounts in your name, defaults on the accounts, or runs up your existing accounts, your credit scores will be damaged. Chapter 10 discusses identity theft, including what to do if you become a victim.

- Pay your debts on time. On-time payments are the best way to improve your Classic FICO scores. The longer your history of on-time payments the better; so if you're behind on any of your accounts, get caught up as quickly as you can.

- Pay down the outstanding credit balances on your credit cards. The higher the balance and the closer you are to your credit limits, the more damage you're doing to your credit scores. Also, accelerate the rate at which you pay off installment loans, such as car loans.

✋ Red Alert!

Paying off a collection account, getting out of bankruptcy, or improving your credit histories in other ways won't increase your credit scores right away because the FCRA says that negative credit record information can be reported for at least seven years. However, the older the information, the less damage it will do to your scores.

- Don't deal with high credit card balances by transferring the debt from one credit card to another in order to take advantage of lower interest rates. Instead, focus on paying off those debts.

- Only apply for credit that you *really* need. Even one application for new credit will lower your Classic FICO somewhat.

- Don't close old accounts, even if you never use them and they have zero balances. The Classic FICO scoring model takes into account how long you've had credit. Yes, having a lot of credit accounts hurts your scores, but once you have them, your scores have already taken a hit.

This chapter marks the end of the "Credit Reporting and Credit Scoring" section of *The Credit Repair Handbook.* After reading this chapter, you should have an appreciation for the importance of credit scores—your three FICO Classic scores in particular. You should also understand the various factors that determine how high or low your scores are and what you can do to increase them.

The next chapter begins the "Rebuilding Your Credit after Serious Money Troubles" section of this book, and will explain what you should do to help ensure that the credit rebuilding process goes smoothly.

✋ Red Alert!

When you are paying for merchandise, resist a retailer's invitation to apply for a store credit card in order to get an immediate discount on your purchase. The discount is not worth the fact that if you open the new account you will harm your credit scores.

Rebuilding Your Credit After Serious Money Troubles

Credit Rebuilding Preliminaries

5

Once your finances have stabilized and you can pay all of your bills, it's time to begin the credit rebuilding process, which is described in this chapter. But before you do, there are some credit rebuilding preliminaries that are a good idea to get out of the way. These preliminaries can help you ensure that the rebuilding process goes smoothly, and can help minimize the likelihood that you'll develop new money problems in the future that will damage your credit histories all over again. This chapter reviews each of these preliminaries and explains why they're important to your financial future.

PRELIMINARY STEPS TO TAKE ON THE ROAD TO CREDIT REBUILDING

The actions on the following list represent the steps you should take in preparation for rebuilding your credit. Take all of the steps that apply to you after reading the extended discussions later in this chapter. Meanwhile, if you still have any open credit accounts, manage them responsibly so that all of the new information that gets added to your credit histories will be positive:

■ Review your Equifax, Experian, and TransUnion credit reports, and do what you can to minimize the impact of any negative information they may contain. You'll learn how to do that in the next section of this chapter. Also, dispute any errors in those credit histories using the investigative process described in chapter 3. The errors can slow or even derail your rebuilding efforts.

■ Set up a household budget and manage your spending according to your budget.

■ Build up your savings.

■ Get clear about why your credit record became damaged so that you can take steps to ensure that history doesn't end up repeating itself.

MINIMIZE THE IMPACT OF NEGATIVE-BUT-TRUE INFORMATION IN YOUR CREDIT HISTORY

Generally there's not much you can do about the negative-but-true information in your credit histories, because the Fair Credit Reporting Act (FCRA) allows most of the information to be reported for seven years, and says that some kinds of negative information can linger even longer (chapter 1 explains how long different types of negative information can be reported). In most instances, you'll just hav e to be patient and remember that with each passing month and year, the significance of the negative information will dwindle in the eyes of creditors and anyone else who reviews your credit histories, especially if all of the new information that you add to those records during the rebuilding process is positive. Eventually, the negative information will drop out of your credit files. However, depending on the nature of the negative-but-true information, and the circumstances surrounding the information, you may be able to lessen its impact on your finances and even make some of the negative information go away by by doing the following:

- Using written statements

- Getting rid of charge-offs

- Settling outstanding debts

- Resolving past-due taxes

✋ Red Alert!

Disreputable credit fix-it organizations adver-tise that they can repair your credit histories by making negative information disappear like magic and by giving you a brand new prob-lem-free credit identity. Watch out!

These firms use illegal methods to do what they promise. If you cooperate with them you may end up violating the law, too. You could even be prosecuted if you're found out.

Explain Negative-but True-Information with a Written Statement

You may be able to lessen the potential impact of some of the nega-tive-but-true information in your credit files by preparing a writ-ten statement of no more than 100 words that explains the reason for the information. Of course, this advice assumes that you have a good explanation. For example, your child was seriously ill and you couldn't pay for her medical care and keep up with all of your finan-cial obligations at the same time; you lost your job and used up your savings while you were trying to find a new one; or your ex-spouse stopped paying your court-ordered child support and you were forced into bankruptcy as a result. Although creditors, insurance companies, employers, and others may be willing to cut you a little slack if they think your explanation is credible, don't expect any breaks from them if your explanation is that you don't have good money-management skills or that you spent too much.

The FCRA does not require the credit reporting agencies (CRAs) to make a statement that explains negative-but-true information a part of your credit files. (It only requires them to include a personal written statement explaining negative information

> **! Hot Tip**
>
> Your written statement will have more credibility if you had a good credit history before the problem that you describe occurred.

you believe is inaccurate, incomplete or too old to be reported that you disputed using the process set out in the FCRA, but were not able to get corrected.) Even so, the CRAs may agree to include it, although it's a long shot—and if they agree, you'll probably have to pay each of them a small fee. However, being able to "tell your side of the story" in your credit history is worth the money.

After you prepare your statement, make a copy for your files and mail it to each of the CRAs, together with a letter requesting that it be included in your credit file. (Figure 5.1 provides a sample letter.) Send it via certified mail with a return receipt requested.

If any of the CRAs agree to your request, order a copy of your credit report(s) a month or two later to make sure the statement is there. If it's not, get back in touch with the relevant CRA.

> **! Hot Tip**
>
> Attach to your letter copies of any documents you may have that support the information in your written statement for example, a copy of your last unemployment check, copies of your child's medical bills, a copy of your child-support court order, and copies of any letters or court documents that prove that you ex has violated the court order.
>
> Whenever you apply for new credit, employment, and so on, it's a good idea to attach to your application a copy of your written statement, and then to follow up by phone or in person to discuss the statement and to answer any questions. Doing this is important because whoever checks your credit history during the application review process may not read the statement.

FIGURE 5.1 Sample Letter Requesting That a Written Statement Be Added to Your Credit History

[Date]

To Whom It May Concern:

I am writing to request that you make the attached statement a part of my credit history so that whoever reviews it has an opportunity to read the statement. It provides an explanation for much of the negative-but-true information in my credit file.

The following information should help you access my credit file:

* [Your full name, including Sr., Jr., III, etc.]
* [Your Social Security number. To help protect you from identity theft, you can request that when the CRA processes your order, the last five numbers of your Social Security number not be printed on your credit report.]
* [Your date of birth]
* [Your spouse's full name, if you are married]
* [Your spouse's Social Security number]
* [Your current address, and your previous address(es) if you've not lived at your present address for at least two years. Include your apartment number or private mailbox number if appropriate.]
* [Your evening and daytime phone numbers, including area codes]

Thank you for assisting me with this request. If you have any questions, please contact me at the phone number listed above.

Sincerely,

[Your signature—sign your name as it appears in your credit history]

Deal with Charge-Offs and Settle Debts for Less

Another way to handle negative-but-true information in your credit history is to try to strike a deal with the creditor or collection agency reporting the information to one or more of the CRAs. Take *charge-offs* for example. An account is reported as a charge-off when the creditor or debt collector to whom you owe the money decides that it's unlikely it can ever collect the money you owe, decides not to keep trying, and writes off the debt. Having a charge-off on your credit history is a big negative, but you may be able to get rid of it. For example, if you can pay the charge-off amount, the creditor or debt collector would begin reporting the debt as a *paid charge-off,* which is slightly better for your credit history than a charge-off, because it shows that you acknowledged that you owed the money and you paid it, albeit late.

❗ Hot Tip

Even better than getting a creditor or debt collector to report a debt that was charged off as a *paid charge-off* after you pay it or settle it for less is for the creditor or collection agency to report the debt as *paid as agreed.* Although the creditor or collection agency is likely to balk at doing that, it never hurts to ask for what you really want.

You can also ask a creditor to report as *paid as agreed* a past-due account that hasn't yet been sent to collections or been written off, in exchange for you paying the full amount that you owe or for settling the debt by paying something less than the full amount due. Again, the creditor may deny your request, but then again it may give you what you're asking for. In other words, it's worth a try.

If you want to get a charge-off removed from your credit history but you can't afford to pay the full amount of the charge-off, another option is to try to settle your debt for less. You can ask that the debt be reported as a paid charge-off. The creditor or collection agency might accept your offer, thinking that getting something on the debt is better than nothing.

If you and a creditor or debt collector come to an agreement about a charge-off, don't pay any money on it until you get the terms of the agreement in writing. If the creditor or debt collector won't put your agreement in writing, prepare a written agreement yourself that spells out everything you both agreed to. Date and sign it and send a copy to the creditor or debt collector via certified mail with a return receipt requested. A month or two later, after you have paid the charge-off, order your credit report from whichever CRA is reporting the debt to be sure that the creditor or the debt collector lived up to its end of the bargain. If your credit history does not reflect the agreed upon change, call the creditor or debt collector and follow up with a letter referencing the terms of your agreement and asking that the creditor or debt collector comply with them. Attach to your letter a copy of the agreement. Send everything certified mail with a return receipt requested.

Clear Up Tax Problems

If your credit histories have been damaged because you didn't pay your state or federal taxes and the taxing authority has a lien on your home or some other real estate you may own, the sooner you can pay the taxes and get the lien removed, the better for your rebuilding efforts. Unpaid tax liens are very damaging to your credit history. Also, the longer you owe past-due taxes, the bigger your tax debt will become, due to interest and penalties.

🖐 Red Alert!

A federal tax lien will stay in your credit histories for 10 years. However, it's likely that the IRS will renew the lien once the 10 years are up, especially if the amount that you owe is substantial. Therefore, the lien could damage your credit histories for decades to come. Meanwhile, as long as there's a lien on the asset, you won't be able to borrow against it, sell it, or transfer the asset to someone else. Also, you must get up-front permission from the IRS before you can sell the asset. If you do, the lien will be released at the sale closing, the title company will pay the IRS what you owe to it, and you'll get whatever money may be left.

If you cannot afford to pay the full amount of an income tax debt in a lump sum, you may be able to arrange to pay it over time through an installment plan. Another option is to settle the debt for less than what you owe on it. To request an installment plan from the IRS, fill out IRS Form 9465, which you can pick up at your local IRS office or download at *www.irs.gov/pub/irs-pdf/f9465.*

If you owe more than $25,000 to the IRS, you'll also have to file IRS Form 433-A. To ask the IRS to settle your debt for less, which is referred to as making an *offer in compromise,* you must complete IRS Form 656 and pay the agency a $150 application fee. You can obtain this form at your local IRS office or at *www.irs.gov/pub/irs-pdf/f656.pdf.*

If you owe back property taxes, the taxing authority may allow you to pay the debt over time. Find out at what point it will release its lien. It may agree to release it as soon as you begin making your payment, although it's more likely that it will either not release the lien until you've paid a certain percentage of your tax debt or until you've paid the tax debt in full.

If you feel uncomfortable dealing with a past-due tax debt on your own, get in touch with a tax attorney or a CPA who has experience negotiating with the taxing authority that put the lien on your property.

Getting professional help is especially important when you're dealing with the IRS because the agency is notoriously difficult to deal with, and the forms you will have to complete in order to get an installment plan—and especially to negotiate an offer in compromise—can be complicated and confusing for the average consumer.

BUDGETING ONCE YOUR HISTORY IS IN GOOD SHAPE

A household budget is an essential money-management tool, whether you're making a bundle of money or just scraping by. Although you may grimace and groan when you read the word *budget,* don't be intimidated—it's nothing more than a written spending plan that helps you control your money. Among other things, a budget helps you do the following:

- Make smart decisions about what you will do with your money every month, including paying your living expenses, paying off your debts, putting money in savings, buying groceries, eating out, building up your retirement fund, and so on. Without a budget, you may spend too much at the start of the month and have to use credit toward the end of the month to help pay for your living expenses, which will undermine your rebuilding efforts.

- Achieve the financial goals that are important to you. You're a lot more likely to turn your goals into realities if you plan for them using a budget than if you just hope that somehow, someday you'll have the money you need.

- Build an emergency fund so that if you are hit with an unexpected expense that you can't afford to pay out of your checking account (like an expensive car repair) you can pay for it with cash, not credit. Also, having an emergency fund makes you less vulnerable financially to life's ups and downs.

If you already have a budget, be sure that it's realistic. In other words, can you really live on your current plan, or are you always coming up short at the end of the month? Also, make sure that you're budgeting not just your regular monthly fixed and variable expenses, but also your periodic expenses, too. Fixed expenses are expenses that are the same month after month— your rent or mortgage payment, for example. Variable expenses are monthly expenses like groceries and gas for your car—they're not always the same amounts every month, but they always exist. Periodic expenses, on the other hand, are expenses that only occur once in a while. Income taxes, prop-

> ❗ **Hot Tip**
>
> A counselor with a nonprofit credit counseling agency can help you evaluate your current budget and identify problems and possible changes. If you don't have a budget, the counselor can help you develop one and teach you how to monitor it each month by comparing what you budgeted to what you actually spent. See chapter 7 for advice about how to find a good credit counseling agency.

erty taxes, and tuition are common examples of periodic expenses. Despite the fact that you don't have to pay your periodic expenses every month, it's a good idea to prorate them by dividing the total amount of each expense by 12 (for 12 months) and then every month to deposit the prorated amount for each expense into your savings account. That way you'll have the money you need to pay your periodic expenses when they come due.

If you don't have a budget, the next several sections of this chapter provide an overview of the budget-building process, together with a sample budget. The resource section at the back of this book provides additional resources for creating a budget and living with one.

BUILDING A BUDGET

The budgeting process has seven steps.

Step #1. Establish your financial goals. You can have short-term, intermediate-term, or long-term goals:

- **Short-term goals** are goals that you believe you can achieve in a year or less. They may include having enough money to pay cash for your children's clothes when it's time for them to start a new school year, or having the money you need to get a secured MasterCard or Visa and/or a secured loan as part of the credit rebuilding process. When you begin that process you may not be able to qualify for a regular MasterCard or Visa card right away, or for even a small, unsecured loan. Instead, you'll have to secure or guarantee payment with money in your savings account. The next chapter provides more detail on getting a secured MasterCard or Visa and a secured bank loan.

- **Intermediate-term goals** are goals that you expect will take between one year and five years to achieve, like paying off your car loan or paying off a credit card.

■ **Long-term goals** are goals that you think will take you more than five years to achieve. Having enough money for a down payment on a home, having enough money to retire, or having enough money to help pay for your child's college education are examples of common long-term goals.

Once you've identified and categorized your goals, figure out the approximate amount of money you'll need to save in order to attain each of the goals on your list within the time frames you've set for yourself. Then, based on the relative importance of each goal to your life, decide how much money you can realistically afford to put toward achieving each goal every month. At first, you may not be able to save anything for some of your goals. But over time, as your finances improve and as you achieve some of your immediate goals, you can begin saving to achieve the others.

Step #2. Figure out your expenses. List all of your expenses and their amounts on a form like the one in Figure 5.2 on page 87 or by using budgeting software like *Quicken Basic or Quicken Deluxe.* Then, total them up. You'll need your checkbook registers, receipts, account statements, online bill-paying records, and any other relevant expense information to complete this exercise. Although the process of identifying all of your expenses and their amounts can be tedious, it's important to be as thorough and accurate as possible. Otherwise, your budget won't be accurate, which means that it won't help you manage your money.

Speaking of being thorough, most people tend to underestimate their spending, especially the amount of cash they spend on miscellaneous items like lattes, snacks, money for the kids, and other everyday expenses. To get a handle on your miscellaneous spending, carry a notebook with you for a few months and write down *every* penny you spend in cash and exactly what you

> **❗ Hot Tip**
>
> Your goals are reflections of your financial situation and of your personal values and priorities. For example, what may be an intermediate goal for you might be a short-term goal for someone else. In other words, there's no right or wrong time frame for achieving your goals.

spend those pennies and dollars on. Your spouse or partner should do the same. Not only will this exercise help you get a more accurate handle on your actual monthly spending, it will also help you pinpoint potential spending cuts if you need to reduce your spending.

Step #3. Record the amount that you want to save each month. Don't get discouraged if you can't save a lot at first. It's more important at first to develop the savings habit by committing to set aside a set amount of money each month, than to worry about how much you're saving. Certainly you should try to save as much as you can, but saving even a small amount on a regular basis is better than not saving at all, and over time those small amounts will add up. When you are recovering from money troubles, saving money may mean making some sacrifices for a while, but the faster you build up your savings account, the sooner you can begin the rebuilding process and the sooner you'll have a financial safety net to protect your finances.

> **❗ Hot Tip**
>
> Financial experts advise that you save at least 10 percent of your net monthly income (monthly take home pay) every month and that you keep enough money in your savings account to cover six to eight months of your living expenses. You may be unable to save that much at first, but as your finances improve, you should be able to come closer and closer to being able to save 10 percent, or even more.

The easiest way to save is to ask your employer to automatically deduct a fixed amount of money from each of your paychecks and to deposit those funds directly into your savings account. If the money isn't included in your take-home pay, you're less apt to miss it, and you don't have to worry about spending it. If you're self-employed, ask your bank to automatically transfer a set amount of money every month from your checking to your savings account.

Step #4. Add up the regular income that comes into your home each month, and record that total as well. Your income may include employment take-home pay, self-employment income, investment income, royalties, child support or spousal support you may receive on a regular basis, and so on.

Step #5. Once you've totaled up all of your expenses per month and all of your income per month, add your total monthly expenses to the total amount you've budgeted for monthly savings. Subtract that total from your total monthly income. The number you end up with will either be a positive or a negative number. A positive number means that you'll have money left over each month if your income, expenses, and savings are the same as what you've written down in your budget. A negative number means that you have a deficit—in other words, your income is less than what you've budgeted for spending and savings.

Step #6. If you have a deficit, try to reduce your expenses. In looking for expenses to cut, focus first on your variable expenses, as those are the expenses over which you have the most control. Your spending notebook should help you identify where you can cut back. It's possible also that you may have to budget less for savings, at least for a while. If spending and/ or saving less don't get rid of your deficit, figure out how to increase your household income. For example, you

> **❗Hot Tip**
>
> If you have trouble developing a workable budget, set up an appointment with a nonprofit credit counseling agency. The counselor can help you figure out ways to reduce your spending so that you can make ends meet, and so that you can start saving. The agency may offer budgeting workshops, as well.

may need to get a second job, or if your spouse or partner doesn't work outside the home, he or she may need to have a paying job for a while. Getting rid of your budget deficit is essential to the success of your credit rebuilding efforts, so do what it takes! Check out the resources section of this book for more help with reducing your spending.

Step #7. Monitor your budget. Post your final budget in a visible location so that you and your spouse or partner will be reminded of it on a daily basis and can easily refer to it during the month to make sure that what you're spending and saving is on track. Then at the end of each month, compare your budgeted amounts to what you actually spent and saved. If some of your expenses were higher than what was budgeted, or if you didn't save as much as you budgeted, figure out why. You may not have budgeted enough for certain expenses.

The amount that you planned on saving may be unrealistic. You may have had to pay an unexpected expense. Maybe you didn't really try to make your budget work that month. As appropriate, make adjustments in your budget and/or in your attitude.

FIGURE 5.2 Sample Monthly Household Budget

If you do not use budgeting software to create your budget, then use this form or create a similar form on your computer. If some of your expenses are not listed on the form, be sure to add them:

Monthly Household Income

Your take-home pay   _____

Your spouse or partner's take-home pay   _____

Child support   _____

Spousal support   _____

Other income   _____

Total Monthly Income   _____

Monthly Expenses

Fixed Expenses

Rent or mortgage payment   _____

Home equity loan payment   _____

Car loan   _____

Monthly insurance payments   _____

Cable   _____

Phone (landline)   _____

Cell phone   _____

Internet service   _____

Child care   _____

Prescription medication   _____

Transportation   _____

Other   _____

Other   _____

Other   _____

Variable Expenses

Utilities   _____

Groceries   .   _____

Credit cards   _____

FIGURE 5.2 continues on next page

FIGURE 5.2 continued from previous page

Entertainment   _____

Dry cleaning   _____

Clothing   _____

Body care   _____

Other   _____

Other   _____

Other   _____

Periodic Expenses

Tuition   _____

Subscriptions   _____

Gifts   _____

License renewal; auto inspection/registration   _____

Property taxes   _____

Income taxes   _____

Other   _____

Other   _____

Other   _____

Total Monthly Expenses   _____

Monthly Contributions to Your Savings   _____

Total Monthly Expenses + Monthly Contributions to Your Savings = _____

Total Monthly Income _____ **– Total Expenses & Contributions** _____ **=** _____

FACE FACTS ABOUT WHY YOUR CREDIT HISTORY GOT DAMAGED

Becoming clear about exactly why your credit history got damaged is another credit rebuilding preliminary. If you don't figure out the cause of your financial problems, history is likely to repeat itself. You don't want to go through the effort of rebuilding your credit record just to have the same problems that ruined it the first time ruin it again.

Possible reasons why your credit history is damaged include the following:

- You don't have good money-management skills. For information about many of the free and low-cost resources available to help you improve your skills, deepen your knowledge of everyday financial management issues, and quickly resolve problems related to your finances, turn to the resources section of this book.

- Saving money has never been a priority in your life. Spending it has been your focus.

- You've bought into our culture's overemphasis on money, material goods, and instant gratification. Chapter 8 discusses this phenomenon.

- You have a spending problem. For example, you spend for emotional reasons—to make yourself feel better, for example—or you can't control your spending. If you have a spending problem, it's critical that you acknowledge and deal with it. (Figure 5.3 highlights the most common signs of a spending problem.) Attending Debtors Anonymous (D.A.) meetings is a great way to overcome this problem. It uses the tried-and-true methods of Alcoholics Anonymous to help overspenders take control of their spending. To find a Debtors Anonymous chapter in your area, go to *www.debtorsanonymous.org* or call 1-781-453-2743. If no D.A. chapter is convenient to you, D.A. also offers meetings by phone and online. To learn about those meetings, go to *www.debtorsanonymous.org/find_meeting/online.*

■ Your divorce devastated your finances and you've been struggling to recover ever since. If you're short of money, finding a better paying job or a second job may be the answer. If you owe too much relative to your income, your best option may be to meet with a consumer bankruptcy attorney. Short of that, some of the resources listed at the back of this book may help you get control of your finances and put an end to your struggles.

If you're not sure what caused the problems that ruined your credit history, schedule an appointment with a reputable nonprofit credit counseling agency—or with a mental health professional, if you think that you may have an unhealthy relationship with money. Chapter 7 tells you how to find a good credit counselor. To locate a good mental health professional, visit a website like *www.findcounseling.com*, or get a referral from close friends or family members who have received therapy and were happy with their therapist.

FIGURE 5.3 Signs That You May Have a Spending Problem

The following list describes some of the signs of a spending problem. The more that apply to you, the more likely that you are a problem spender. Swallow your pride and get help—if you don't, the problem will continue to sabotage your life in many ways, including undermining your credit rebuilding efforts. For more information about the characteristics of overspenders, visit the Debtors Anonymous Web site at *www.debtorsanonymous.org*.

- You're not sure how many credit accounts you have and how much you owe on each account.

- You don't know the amounts of your monthly expenses or other details related to your financial life.

- You are always in a state of financial crisis. For example, your accounts are overdrawn, your checks bounce, you are short the money you need to pay an important debt such as your mortgage or car loan, debt collectors are calling, you're constantly "robbing Peter to pay Paul," and so on.

- You have a live-for-today attitude. It's important to appreciate every day in your life, but not at the expense of planning your financial future or putting money in savings.

- You spend money you don't have, even though you know that you shouldn't, given the possible consequences.

- You make purchases you don't need just so you can buy more things. In fact, the sales tags may still be attached to some of the items you've purchased.

- Your spending has created tension between you and your spouse or partner, and/or it's created bad feelings between you and your friends and family, maybe because they're tired of lending you money and not getting paid back.

- You experience a high after you spend money, and especially after you use credit.

- You are secretive about your spending. For example, you try to hide your credit card bills from your spouse or partner and you sneak your purchases into your home.

- You feel badly after you overspend, but you do it again, and again, and again anyway.

This chapter discussed the various actions you should take to help ensure that the credit rebuilding process goes smoothly. Once you've gotten all of the credit rebuilding preliminaries out of the way, you're ready to start the rebuilding process. The next chapter guides you through that process step by step.

Going Through the
Credit Rebuilding Process

6

Once you've gotten the preliminaries out of the way by following the advice in chapter 5, you're ready to begin the credit rebuilding process. The process isn't difficult or complicated—it's a matter of adding positive information to your credit files over time by obtaining small amounts of new credit and managing it responsibly. Gradually, as the amount of positive information increases, and as the negative information in your credit files begins to drop off because the information becomes too old to be reported, your credit histories will start to improve and your credit scores will begin to rise.

There is no one right way to rebuild your credit. However, the process described in this chapter has worked well for my clients over the years. I feel confident that it will work equally well for you.

WHEN TO START REBUILDING AND WHAT TO EXPECT

You can start rebuilding your credit as soon as your financial situation has stabilized and you are able to pay all of your bills on time. At the beginning of the process, the more damaged your credit history, the less likely that you'll qualify for low-interest or unsecured credit—much less for a large loan like a mortgage. Over time, however, as you mange your credit responsibly it will become easier to obtain credit at reasonable terms and to qualify for unsecured credit, and even a mortgage. It's a matter of regaining the trust of creditors by establishing a pattern of responsible credit management.

During the credit rebuilding process, don't apply for a lot of credit. Only apply for the credit you really need. If you look too eager to have credit again, creditors will see that as a sign that you may be headed for more financial trouble. Also, having a lot of credit-related inquiries in your credit histories will lower your credit scores.

> **! Hot Tip**
>
> If you've not already begun putting money in savings, start now! You will probably need the cash at the beginning of the credit rebuilding process, because most reputable creditors won't give you new credit at first unless you can secure it (guarantee payment) with either money in a savings account or with a certificate of deposit (CD) that you purchase with that money.
>
> The interest rate on savings accounts and CDs varies from bank to bank, so shop around for the best rate. The higher the rate, the faster your money will grow. The website Bankrate.com is a good resource.

ADD POSITIVE MISSING INFORMATION TO YOUR CREDIT FILES

One way to improve your credit histories sooner rather than later is to add positive information about accounts that are not being reported. For example, when you reviewed your credit histories you may have noticed information about a loan you have with a local independent bank or an account with a local retailer was missing. These types of creditors, as well as some oil and gas companies, credit unions, and others, may not report consumer account payment information to the credit reporting agencies (CRAs), or may only report information when consumers default on their obligations to them (when they've turned an account over to collections or when they've written off a debt as uncollectible).

If you find that some of your credit accounts are not being reported to the CRAs—assuming your payment history on the accounts is good—write to each of the CRAs and ask them to add the missing information to your credit files. Attach to your letters copies of your most recent statements for each of the accounts you want added. Although the CRAs are not required to comply with your request, they may after verifying your account information. You probably will have to pay them a fee for each insertion. Also, be prepared to contact the CRAs several times in order to get an answer one way or another in response to your requests.

If you cannot get the CRAs to agree to add missing account information to your credit files, another option is to approach the creditor that isn't reporting the information and request that it provide the CRAs with your account payment history. Put your request in writing.

A third option for getting missing information added to your credit histories is to enlist the help of a consumer law attorney who has specific experience with the *Fair Credit Reporting Act*. Because the attorney will be more familiar with all of the provisions of the law and their fine points, she may be able to figure out a way to get the information into your credit files.

If none of these approaches works, you can prepare a written statement about the missing account information, and whenever you apply for important credit or employment, you can attach that statement to your application along with proof that the information in the statement is accurate (such as a statement from the creditor that you've always paid your account on time, that you paid the loan in full, and so on).

Be aware of a couple caveats associated with adding missing accounts to your credit files. First, the information probably won't be as important to potential creditors as having positive information in your credit histories regarding your payment histories on a MasterCard or Visa, or on a mortgage with a major bank. Also, because the creditors associated with the accounts you want added don't report consumer account information regularly to the CRAs, whatever you can get added will be a one-time addition. However, any positive information that you can get into your credit history is better than having no positive information in it at all.

APPLY FOR A BANK LOAN

Once you've cleared up any problems in your credit files and have a couple thousand dollars in savings, apply for a small bank loan. The amount of the loan you qualify for will depend in part on the information in the credit histories the lender reviews to evaluate your application and on the lending policies of the bank. Realistically, however, if your credit is ruined, the most you'll probably be able to borrow at first will be between $500 and $1,000. Even so, getting even a small loan is an important step in the credit rebuilding process.

If you have an established relationship with a bank, then meet with a loan officer at that bank to discuss your interest in borrowing money. If you don't have an established relationship with a bank, then meet with a loan officer at the bank where your savings account is located. During your meeting, be up front about the fact you have had financial troubles in the past (the loan officer will figure that out soon enough after reviewing your credit files). Let the loan officer know that you are in the process of rebuilding your credit, and as a part of that process you would like a small bank loan. Explain why your money problems developed, assuming your explanation is sympathetic, and let the loan officer know what you've done to minimize the possibility that you'll develop more problems in the future—you've established a regular savings plan, taken a money-management class, your spouse

---

🤚 **Red Alert!**

Don't go into any more detail than you have to about your past financial troubles when you meet with a loan officer, but if he or she asks you questions about your money problems, don't be evasive. If you are, you may appear untrustworthy and could jeopardize your chances for a loan as a result.

or partner is now working outside the home, you're living on a budget, and so on.

Although the idea of meeting with a loan officer may sound intimidating, loan officers are ordinary people just like you and me. Most of them don't have big fancy offices or earn big bucks. Some of them may even have experienced their own financial troubles, so they'll understand what you've gone through and why you want to rebuild your credit. A face-to-face meeting with a loan officer can help improve your chances of getting a loan because you won't be just some faceless loan application, but a real person with a story to tell. Also, a face-to-face meeting gives you an opportunity to establish a good rapport with the loan officer and to get your questions answered.

> **❢ Hot Tip**
>
> Dress neatly and conservatively for your meeting. Don't wear cutoffs, torn jeans, or T-shirts, and avoid flashy jewelry.

IF THE FIRST LOAN OFFICER SAYS NO

If the first loan officer you meet with turns you down for a loan, politely ask why and find out what you need to do in order to get one. The loan officer may tell you that you need more money in savings, that your financial troubles are too recent and more time needs to pass now that they're over, or that you need more income. Take the loan officer's advice to heart, because other loan officers are likely to turn you down for similar reasons. When you are ready, schedule a meeting with a loan officer at a different bank.

If you can't find a loan officer willing to give you a loan right now, be patient. Follow the advice they may have provided regarding how to make yourself more attractive as a borrower, and continue managing your finances responsibly. If you follow this advice, you will qualify for a loan eventually.

When you are approved for a loan, it will probably be a *secured loan*. In other words, the lender will want you to guarantee that it will get paid back either by opening a savings account at the bank and keeping a certain amount of money in the account or by purchasing a CD for a certain amount from the bank. Then, if you don't repay the loan according to the terms of your agreement with the lender, it can take that money, which is referred to as your loan *collateral*. While you are paying off the loan, you won't have access to those funds.

WHAT TO DO AFTER YOU'VE PAID OFF YOUR FIRST LOAN

Once you've paid off your first loan, order copies of your credit reports from the CRAs to which the bank reports so you can be sure that the information in your credit file(s) is complete and accurate. If it's not, correct the information following the directions in chapter 3 before you apply for additional credit.

Next, apply to the same lender for a second loan. This time, ask for an *unsecured loan.* If the lender turns you down, you can either apply to a different lender for an unsecured loan or you can ask the first lender for a second secured loan that is larger than your first loan. Whatever you do, make all of the payments on your second loan on time and in full. Again, once you've paid off the loan, check your credit record(s) to confirm that the information shows the loan was paid off according to the terms of your loan agreement.

If your second loan was secured, try again to get an unsecured loan after you've repaid the second loan. Eventually you will qualify for one, assuming you continue to manage your finances responsibly.

APPLY FOR A VISA OR MASTERCARD

Either at the same time that you apply for your first bank loan or sometime later, apply for a Visa or MasterCard. Depending on the condition of your credit histories, you may not be able to qualify for a regular unsecured bank card right at first, which means that you'll have to apply for a secured card instead. However, if you manage the secured card responsibly, eventually you'll qualify for an unsecured MasterCard or Visa.

Understanding How Secured Credit Cards Work

A secured MasterCard or Visa looks just like any other MasterCard or Visa, so no one will know that you couldn't qualify for a regular card. However, there are some important differences between the two types of cards.

- Before you can use a secured card, you must deposit a certain amount of money in a savings account that you set up at the bank that issued you the card, or you must purchase a CD for a certain amount from the bank. The money in your savings account or the CD will collateralize your account purchases, so you can't use it—not even to make payments on your account. The value of the collateral will usually range from between a couple hundred dollars to a couple thousand dollars.

- Secured cards tend to have smaller credit limits than unsecured cards. When you're approved for a secured card, the card's credit limit will be a percentage of the value of your collateral—usually between 50 percent and 100 percent of that value. If you make all of your card payments on time, the card issuer may agree to increase your credit limit—although to get the increase, you may have to put up more collateral. If you don't keep up with your card payments, however, the bank will take some or all of your collateral, depending on how much you owe on the account. The bank may close your credit card account, as well.

- Compared to unsecured MasterCards and Visas, secured cards tend to have higher interest rates and higher fees.

! Hot Tip

The websites CardWeb.com and Bankrate.com are two good resources for finding a secured MasterCard or Visa with attractive terms.

You can use your secured credit card to rebuild your credit in one of the following two ways:

1. Each month, use the card to buy things you need, like gasoline for your car or groceries, and then pay off the card balance in full when you receive your statement.

2. Use the card to make a large purchase that you can't afford to repay in full when your account is due. Then pay off the account over time, but as quickly as you can so you don't pay a lot in interest on the outstanding balance. Once you've paid off the card, use it to purchase something else and repeat the same process.

Be sure to compare card offers—regardless of whether you are in the market for a secured or unsecured MasterCard or Visa—because some offers have better terms of credit than others. For example, some cards have lower interest rates than others and some cards have fewer and lower fees. Although you won't be able to qualify for the best terms of credit right away, you should try to get the most attractive card possible. Eventually, regardless of how you use your secured card, you'll be able to qualify for an unsecured MasterCard or Visa, assuming you've managed the secured card responsibly. For general information about how to shop for any kind of credit card, secured or unsecured, see chapter 8. Figure 6.1 fills you in on the additional specific criteria to consider when you're evaluating offers for secured cards in particular.

! Hot Tip

If you receive a pre-approved offer in the mail for a MasterCard or Visa, the bank that sent you the offer provided a list of criteria to one of the CRAs and asked it to review its information in order to determine which consumers in its database met the criteria. Therefore, the card offer may be the best you can qualify for right now. However, make sure it's really a good deal before you accept the offer, and be aware that the creditor is entitled to change the offer—make it somewhat less attractive—after it reviews the details of your credit history and/or checks out your credit score.

FIGURE 6.1 Considerations When You're in the Market for a Secured MasterCard or Visa

Like any other kind of credit card, some secured MasterCards and Visa cards have better terms than others. Therefore, when you are in the market for a secured card, shop for the best deal by considering the following factors:

■ Whether you must pay a fee to apply for the card, the amount of the fee, and whether it's refundable if your card application is denied.

■ The amount of your credit limit.

■ How much money you must give the bank as collateral.

■ The interest rate the CD will earn if you use it to collateralize the card. If the card issuer requires that you open a savings account with it, find out the interest rate on the account.

■ Whether you can increase your credit limit and under what circumstances. Most likely you will have to establish a pattern of on-time card payments before your credit limit can be increased. Also, find out if you'll have to give the bank additional collateral in order to get the increase and the amount of the collateral.

■ When the card issuer can take your collateral.

■ Whether you can get your collateral back if you or the bank closes your account, and under what circumstances.

■ The interest rate the bank will charge if you carry a balance on the card from month to month.

■ The card's grace period (the amount of time you have to pay the card's balance in full before you will be charged interest). If you expect to carry a balance on the card from time to time, avoid secured cards that don't have a grace period.

■ Whether you must pay an application and fee, and whether that fee is refundable if you're turned down for the card. Some card issuers require that you pay hundreds of dollars in up-front fees.

■ What other fees are associated with the card and the amount of each fee.

■ Whether you can convert the card to an unsecured card and the terms of the conversion— when you can covert, whether you must pay a conversion fee, the interest rate on the unsecured card, the card's credit limit, and so on.

USING GASOLINE CARDS AND RETAIL CHARGE CARDS TO REBUILD YOUR CREDIT

Another way to help rebuild your credit histories is to apply for a credit card from one of the major oil and gasoline companies—such as Chevron or Exxon—and for a credit card with a major retailer. These kinds of cards tend to be easy to qualify for but they also tend to have relatively high interest rates. Therefore, if you use them try not charge more than you can afford to pay in full each month.

🖐 Red Alert!

Don't apply for a lot of MasterCards or Visa cards, or for numerous oil and gas cards and retail charge cards. Just one or two MasterCards or Visa cards and one or two oil and gas and retail charge cards are plenty. Applying for a lot of cards will undermine your credit rebuilding efforts because creditors will assume that you are trying to get too much new credit and that you may run up the balances on all of those cards and develop money troubles again.

CREDIT CARD OFFERS TO AVOID

If you are really eager to have credit again, you may be susceptible to credit card scams like newspaper and TV ads or email offers that promise you a credit card, no questions asked, even if your credit history is ruined. The ads may lead you to believe that all you have to do to get the credit card is to call the phone number listed in the ad. Getting credit from a legitimate creditor is never that easy, because legitimate credit card companies will review your credit file before they approve you for a card. In other words, promises of easy credit are sure signs of a scam.

If you call the number listed in one of these ads, it may be a *900 number*, which means that the card advertiser is charging you for the call—probably by the minute—and therefore has a financial incentive to keep you on the line as long as possible. The longer the call, the more money it makes. If you are directed to leave your name and address so that information about the card or a card application can be mailed to you, you may receive a list of banks that offer secured cards—a list that you could put together for yourself for free with just a little time and effort using resources on the Internet—or you may be instructed to return your completed application with an up-front application fee. If you pay the fee, you may not receive a credit card in return, or the card you are sent will come with a very high interest rate and/or a lot of expensive fees. Also, you may only be able to use the card to purchase merchandise from the card issuer's catalog—merchandise that will probably be too expensive and poorly made. On top of that, it's likely that the company that gives you the card won't report information about your payment history to any of the CRAs.

The federal government has established rules for companies that use 900 numbers in order to protect consumers who call them. Figure 6.2 reviews these rules.

> ## ❗ Hot Tip
>
> Before you apply for a gasoline card or a retail store charge card, make sure that the creditor will report your account payment information to at least one of the CRAs. Remember, your goal is to rebuild your credit by adding positive account information to your credit files, not to get a lot of credit again. In fact, applying for too much new credit will harm your credit rebuilding efforts.

FIGURE 6.2 Requirements for 900 Number Advertisers

The Federal Trade Commission (FTC) requires all companies that advertise 900 numbers to indicate the following information in their ads in order to help consumers understand the cost of calling the number. If a company's ad does not include all of this information, steer clear!

- If you will be charged a flat fee for making the call. The fee could be $50 or even higher.
- The per-minute rate for the call, if you will be charged by the minute, and any minimum charge you may have to pay. Also, the ad must indicate the total cost of the call if the advertiser knows its duration in advance.
- The range of fees, if there are different rates for different calling options.
- The cost of any other 900 numbers to which you may be transferred.
- Any additional fees associated with the 900 number call that you may have to pay.

The FTC requires that all of the information on the preceding list be clear and obvious—not hidden in small print—and that the cost of the call be listed next to the 900 number and printed in a size that's at least half the size of the number. If the ad is running on television, it must also disclose an audio cost. In addition, if the cost of calling a 900 number is greater than $2, the cost must be disclosed at the start of your call, and then you must be given time to hang up in order to avoid any charges.

🤚 Red Alert!

An ad for a credit card scam is *unlikely* to explain the various types and amounts of the fees associated with the card, the amount of collateral required if the ad is for a secured credit card, or the interest rate on the card.

OTHER REBUILDING STRATEGIES

Using a cosigner to obtain credit and becoming an authorized user on someone else's credit account are two other ways to begin adding positive information to your credit files. However, there are drawbacks associated with each method.

Use a Cosigner to Get Credit

If you can't qualify for a loan or a credit card on your own right away, you may want to ask a close friend or family member to cosign for the credit. However, as your cosigner, that person will be as responsible as you will be for repaying the debt, which means that if you don't keep up with your card payments, the creditor is legally entitled to look to your cosigner for the money. Therefore, the danger in using a cosigner should be obvious—your relationship with one another may be ruined if you default on the debt and your cosigner has to pay it.

Another cosigning danger is that if you fall behind on the debt, the negative account information will end up not only in your credit files but in the credit files of your cosigner, too. Also, it's possible that having to pay your debt could put your cosigner in a serious financial bind, and maybe even help push him into bankruptcy!

> 🖐 **Red Alert!**
>
> Before you ask someone to cosign for you, make sure that the creditor will report payment information on the credit in both your names, not just in the name of the cosigner.

Given the possible consequences of using a cosigner to obtain new credit, don't use one unless you are sure that you can keep up with your account payments. Also, before the cosigner signs any paperwork related to the debt, be 100 percent up front with him or her about the potential risks of cosigning.

Become an Authorized User on Someone Else's Credit Card

When you become an authorized user on someone else's account, that person, probably a friend or relative, adds your name to the account. In turn, you get access to the credit (assuming the account holder requests that you be issued a credit card), but you aren't responsible for paying on the account. Even so, information about the account will start showing up in the credit file(s) of whichever CRA(s) the account payments are reported to, although the information will note that you are an *authorized user,* which won't carry quite as much weight with future potential creditors as if the card were in your name.

❗ Hot Tip

One way to protect your friend or family member from the downside of cosigning is for you to secure the debt by giving the cosigner a lien on one of your assets. Then, if you don't keep up with your payment obligations and the creditor looks to your cosigner, he or she can take the asset as compensation for having to pay what you owe.

Before you ask someone to let you be an authorized user on a credit card account, make sure he is a good money manager. If he is late with account payments, goes over his credit limit, or stops paying on the account, that information will show up in your credit history, too, which will set back your credit rebuilding efforts.

🤚 **Red Alert!**

If someone lets you become an authorized user on her credit account and gives you a credit card to use, avoid misunderstandings and bad feelings by having a clear and up-front understanding with her about how much you can charge on the card each month and your responsibilities for helping to pay the account.

In this chapter, you learned when you can begin the credit rebuilding process and exactly what the process involves. The next chapter will guide you if you don't feel confident trying to rebuild your own credit and you want professional help. It warns you about credit repair scams and tells you how to find reputable credit rebuilding help.

Getting Credit Rebuilding Help If You Need It

7

If you don't feel confident about your credit rebuilding abilities, or if you would like help with some specific aspect of the process, it's important that you seek help from a reputable rebuilding resource. Beware—you may get ripped off if you don't choose carefully. If that happens, not only will you not have received the help you need, you may also end up out a considerable amount of money and maybe even in legal hot water!

This chapter tells you how to find reliable, low-cost/no-cost credit rebuilding assistance and educates you about the signs that an organization may be a scam. It also reviews your rights under the federal Credit Repair Organizations Act and tells you what to do if you do get scammed by a bogus credit fix-it outfit.

FINDING CREDIBLE CREDIT REBUILDING HELP

If you feel daunted by the prospect of having to rebuild your own credit, if your confidence when it comes to your finances is at an all-time low because of the financial problems in your recent past, or if you've started the credit rebuilding process but have hit a roadblock and want some advice about what to do next, the following are some good options:

- Schedule an appointment with a reputable nonprofit credit counseling agency. Read on to learn how to find one.

- Find out if a local bank or credit union offers a low-cost/no-cost seminar on credit rebuilding, or enroll in a class on the subject offered by a college, university, or continuing education program in your area. Getting some additional education on the subject can help boost your credit rebuilding confidence.

- Locate a consumer law or consumer bankruptcy attorney in your area who offers credit rebuilding advice and assistance. However, it's likely that the help you receive from an attorney's office will be more expensive than what you may have to pay for similar assistance from a nonprofit credit counseling agency.

Find a Good Credit Counseling Agency

Credit counseling agencies offer a wide variety of services to consumers who need help managing their finances, including credit rebuilding assistance. Although there are for-profit and nonprofit credit counseling agencies, whenever possible, work with one that is nonprofit—you'll pay less for the help you need and the counselors who work for nonprofit agencies tend to be better trained. Many for-profit credit counseling agencies are a lot more interested in making money than in helping you, and some of them are little more than scams.

> **✋ Red Alert!**
>
> Some disreputable for-profit credit counseling agencies deliberately chose names in order to appear as though they are nonprofit organizations.

The best way to locate a credit counseling agency that you can trust is to visit the website of the National Foundation for Credit Counseling (NFCC) at *www.nfcc.org*. The organization is the nation's largest network of nonprofit credit counseling organizations, and numerous local credit counseling agencies around the country are affiliated with it. You can also call the NFCC at 1-800-388-2227 to get the name and contact information for an NFCC affiliate near you. If there's no NFCC-affiliated credit counseling agency in your area, look for a nonprofit credit counseling agency that's affiliated with the Association of Independent Consumer Credit Counseling Agencies (AICCCA) by going to *www.aicca.org* or calling 1-703-934-6118.

If you can't find a nonprofit credit-counseling agency affiliated with either the NFCC or the AICCCA that is located close to your home or work, you may be able to get the help from one of the agencies by telephone or online. Also, check your local Yellow Pages for nonprofit credit counseling agencies in your area that are not affiliated with either organization. Then use the questions in the next section to make sure that the agency is reputable and will provide you with the help that you need.

> **❗ Hot Tip**
>
> Once you find a credit couseling agancy to work with, check to see if it's on the list of credit counseling agencies that have been approved by the federal government by going to *www.usdoj. gov/ust/eo/bapcpa/ccde/de_approved*. Although being on the list is not a sure-fire guarantee than an agency will be truly helpful to you, it does provide another level of quality assurance.

Questions to Ask a Nonprofit Credit Counseling Agency Before You Work with It

Before you pay a credit counseling agency any money or sign any paperwork, set up an appointment with an agency counselor in order to get more information about how the agency works, what you can expect if you hire the agency to help you rebuild your credit, and the cost of its services. If you can't meet in person, get this same information by telephone and then ask that the agency also send you the information in writing.

Get clear and complete answers to the following questions when you speak with a credit counselor:

- Do you regularly help consumers rebuild their credit histories?

- What kinds of help do you provide?

- How do you charge for your services?

- Will I have to pay you any money up front, and if I do, how much will I have to pay?

- If I decide to work with you, do you have a written contract that I will have to sign? (Ask to see a copy of the contract and read it carefully. Among other things, the contact should spell out the specific services the agency will provide; a time frame for their delivery; the total amount of money that you will be charged, and when the money will be due; as well as whether you can cancel the contract, and under what conditions, and whether you can get all or a portion of the money back that you may have paid if you cancel.)

🖐 Red Alert!

If an agency tells you that it doesn't use contracts, find another agency to work with. A reputable organization will want to put all of the terms of your agreement in writing.

- Do you have printed information about your credit rebuilding services that you can share with me? (A reputable agency should have this information.)

- What kind of training do counselors with your agency receive?

- Will I be assigned a specific counselor to work with? (The answer should be yes.)

- What will be my obligations if I decide to work with your agency?

- Are you affiliated with a national network of credit counseling agencies? (If the agency says that it is, contact the national network to confirm that fact. If the agency is not affiliated with a national network, it's probably safe to assume that the agency isn't nonprofit, even if its name makes it sound like it is.)

- Do you have a performance bond? When an organization has purchased an insurance bond from a bonding company, the bond ensures that you can get your money back if the agency does not provide you with the services for which you paid.

When you find an agency that you want to work with, ask for the names and phone numbers of consumers the organization has helped in the past and then call those individuals. If they all tell you pretty much the same exact thing or seem to mimic what the credit counselor told you or the wording in any printed materials, they may be agency employees or people the organization has paid to say good things about it. Don't work with the agency.

Other Ways to Make Sure that You Hire the Right Credit Counseling Agency

There are other things you can do to make sure that you work with a reputable credit counseling agency. For example, it's a good idea to contact each of the following organizations, because all maintain records of consumer complaints against various businesses and non-profit organizations, including complaints against credit counseling agencies. If the credit counseling agency you are thinking about working with has a history of complaints, find a different agency:

- **The Better Business Bureau (BBB).** You can locate contact information for the BBB in your area by looking it up in the business pages of your local phone book or by using the BBB directory on the website of the national Better Business Bureau at *www.bbb.org.*

- **The consumer protection office of your state attorney general's office.** The phone number for this office should be listed in the Blue Pages of your local phone book. You can also obtain contact information for that office by going to *www.naag.org,* the Web site of the National Association of Attorneys General.

- **Your state's banking commission or department of banking.** In some states, these offices maintain records of complaints against credit counseling agencies.

❗Hot Tip

When you contact your state attorney general's office, find out if your state requires credit counseling agencies operating in your state to be accredited. If that's the case, get the name of the accrediting organization and contact it to make certain that the agency you are thinking about working with has the appropriate accreditation.

If you will be getting credit rebuilding assistance from a credit counseling agency over the phone or online, contact the BBB in the area where the agency is located. Also contact the consumer protection office of the attorney general in the state where the agency is located, and find out if that state's banking commission or department of banking maintains complaint record on credit counseling agencies.

RECOGNIZING A CREDIT REPAIR RIP-OFF

If you don't adequately screen the credit counseling organization you decide to work with, you may end up with one that preys on naïve and uninformed consumers who don't realize that they can rebuild their own credit histories for little or no money. Some of these outfits make big promises that can sound really attractive if you are desperate for new credit, such as "Make all of the negative information in your credit history disappear!" or "A bankruptcy in your credit history? No problem!" or "Use little-known loopholes in the Fair Credit Reporting Act (FCRA) to get rid of negative credit record information." They may even give you a money-back guarantee.

Falling for the promises of a disreputable credit repair organization can be costly in more ways than one. For example, it may do the following:

- Take your money—maybe as much as $1,000!—and in return do little or nothing to help you. For your money, you may end up with nothing more than a list of banks that offer secured credit cards (information that you can get yourself for free on the Internet) or copies of the credit reporting agency (CRA) dispute forms that the repair organization tells you to fill out yourself. You may even get nothing in return, because once you pay the credit repair organization it disappears.

> ✋ **Red Alert!**
>
> Some organizations that claim to be able to help you repair your credit history are actually in the business of stealing your personal information and then selling it to people who want to create new identities for themselves. If your identity is stolen, rebuilding your credit will be difficult, if not impossible, until you undo the damage that the identity thief has caused to your finances. Chapter 10 discusses ways of dealing with identity theft problems.

- Use illegal methods like *skin shedding* or *file segregation* in order to try to trick a creditor into thinking that you're not who you

Red Alert!

If you put false information on a credit application you are committing fraud, which is against the law. The same is true if you obtain an EIN under false pretenses and use it to get credit. If you are criminally prosecuted for what you have done and found guilty, you may have to spend time in prison.

really are but instead someone with an unblemished credit history. Here's how the technique works: the credit repair outfit tells you to apply to the federal government for an Employer Identification Number (EIN) and to use it rather than your Social Security number whenever you apply for new credit, employment, and so on. It may also suggest other things you should do to falsify your credit application, like use a different address than the one you would normally use.

■ Try to take advantage of the provision in the FCRA that says that if you dispute information in your credit file and the CRA (or the information provider) can't confirm the veracity of the information within 30 days, the information must be deleted from your credit file or changed as per your investigation request, even if the information is complete and accurate. To take advantage of this provision, the organization may challenge all of the negative information in your credit file, accurate or not, in order to try to overwhelm the CRA so that it can't possibly investigate everything within the 30-day period. This technique has several problems, however. First, the CRA may realize what's going on and refuse to investigate. Second, even if the CRA does investigate and negative-but-true information is deleted from your credit history as a result, when the provider of the information later confirms that the information is in fact accurate, the information will be put back into your credit file. Third, now that all of the consumer information in a CRA's database is computerized and computers handle many disputes, it's not as easy as it used to be to overwhelm a CRA with a lot of investigation requests.

Red Alert!

If you begin using an EIN rather than your Social Security number at work, you won't continue earning Social Security benefits on your income.

Other credit repair schemes to avoid include the following:

- Ads claiming that if you call a 900 number, you'll learn how to repair your credit history. What the ad may not make clear is that the call will be on your dime and that the longer you're on the line, the more money the organization you've called is making from you.

- An organization that offers to clean up your credit *and* get you new credit, including a credit card, a bank loan, or even a mortgage. The credit you get will have very unattractive terms.

- Organizations that claim that they have a special relationship with the CRAs, so that they can do things that you can't, like get negative-but-accurate information removed from your credit history. They're lying! The FCRA, not the CRAs or credit repair organizations, determine how long negative information can stay in your credit files. Also, credit fix-it organizations cannot do anything that you can't do for yourself.

> ✋ **Red Alert!**
>
> Some disreputable credit repair organizations may advise you to pay a debt you owe in exchange for getting the creditor to agree to stop reporting the negative information related to the debt to the CRAs. Striking such a deal is a legitimate way to rebuild your credit, but you don't need to pay someone else to do it for you. You can do it yourself for free, or a reputable nonprofit credit counseling agency can help you for little or no money, depending on your household income.

> ✋ **Red Alert!**
>
> If you respond to an ad telling you to call a 900 number, do not share any personal or financial information with the person on the other end of the line. It's possible that the ad may be a ruse to steal your identity.

YOUR RIGHTS UNDER THE PROTECTIONS OF THE CREDIT REPAIR ORGANIZATIONS ACT

Credit repair scams have been such a problem that Congress passed the *Credit Repair Organizations Act* (CROA) in 1996. (You'll find a copy of this law at *www.ftc.gov/os/statutes/croa/croa.htm*.) The CROA protects you by spelling out the things that organizations in the business of repairing consumers' credit histories can't and must do. It also gives you certain rights if you are ripped off by an organization. The law does *not* apply to credit repair organizations that are operating as nonprofits.

The CROA says that a credit repair organization must do the following:

- Give you a copy of a standardized disclosure statement titled *Consumer Credit File Rights under State and Federal Law* before you sign a contract for services. The statement explains that you have the right to dispute inaccurate or incomplete information in your credit history on your own, and the right to order copies of your own credit files from each of the CRAs. It also provides you with an overview of your legal rights when you work with a credit repair organization, including the right to sue the organization if it violates any of those rights.

- Give you a written contract that spells out the specific services it will provide to you and their costs. The contract must also tell you how long it will take to provide those services. Any and all promises the organization makes you must be detailed in the contract, too. Also, the contract must list the organization's name and address.

OTHER CROA PROTECTIONS FOR CONSUMERS

The CROA protects you in other ways. For example, a credit repair organization must do the following:

- It must give you a three-day *cooling off* period after you sign its contract. During this time, you can cancel the contract, no questions asked. However, you must cancel by filling out and returning a cancellation form that the credit repair firm should have given you. During the three-day period, the firm cannot provide you with any services.

- It cannot take any money from you or charge you in any way until it provides you with all of the services spelled out in its contract.

- It cannot mislead or deceive you by making false claims about what it can do for you. It also may not mislead you about the legality of actions it may tell you it will take in order to rebuild your credit—for example, it cannot tell you that skin shedding is legal. It cannot encourage you to change your identity in order to get new credit.

MORE ADVICE ABOUT HOW TO PROTECT YOURSELF

If you decide to get help rebuilding your credit, besides following the advice you've received in this chapter so far and being aware of your rights under the CROA, the following are a few other things you can do to protect yourself:

- If you are considering working with an organization that's not covered by the CROA, don't sign its contract unless the contract includes all of the same information that the CROA requires.

- Read carefully any contract you are asked to sign, and don't sign it until you are sure you understand exactly what services you will be provided and how much they will cost, how quickly the services will be provided, and whether you can get your money back and under what circumstances, among other things. If you don't understand something in the contract and you can't get a clear answer from the organization—or it avoids answering your question—don't sign the contract.

- If the organization claiming it can help you rebuild your credit history is located nearby but it refuses to meet with you in person, look for another organization.

WHAT TO DO IF YOU'RE THE VICTIM OF A CREDIT REPAIR SCAM

If a credit repair organization takes advantage of you, file a complaint against the organization with the Federal Trade Commission (FTC). If it receives a lot of complaints about the same company, the FTC will take legal action against it. Chapter 1 explains how to file a complaint with the FTC.

You should also consult with a consumer law attorney, because you may have cause for a lawsuit. You can sue a credit repair organization for actual damages or for the amount of money that you have paid to it—whichever is greater. You can also sue for punitive damages, and for your attorney's fees and court costs associated with your lawsuit. You must file your lawsuit no later than five years after your rights are violated.

This is the final chapter in the "Rebuilding Your Credit after Serious Money Troubles" section of this book. Now it's time to turn your attention to the chapters in the last section of the book, "After You Finally Have It: Protecting Your Good Credit." The first chapter in that section will explain how to minimize the likelihood that future money troubles will ruin your new and improved credit histories.

> **❗ Hot Tip**
>
> Many states have their own credit repair laws, some of which offer consumers more rights. Check with your state attorney general's office to find out if your state is one of them.

After You Finally Have It: Protecting Your Good Credit

Avoiding Financial Problems in the Future

8

After you've begun rebuilding your credit history, the last thing you want is for it to become damaged again. Although there's nothing you can do to provide yourself with a 100 percent guarantee that your financial life will be smooth sailing from here on out, you can do things to help make that prospect more likely, including evaluating your relationship with money and changing it as necessary, becoming a more informed money manager, and learning more about the consumer laws that protect you and how to exercise your legal rights.

To help you accomplish all of the above, this chapter discusses some of the money mind-sets that may have gotten you into financial hot water and that may get you there again if you don't change your thinking. It provides you with important information about the different kinds of credit and how to compare credit offers; reviews many factors that creditors will consider when you apply for new or additional credit; lays out nine money-management rules of thumb to apply to your own finances; and educates you about the ins and outs of various federal consumer protection laws, explaining your rights and responsibilities according to each law, and your options if any of your rights are violated. The information in this chapter, together with the information in chapters 5 and 9, provides you with a basic primer on sound money management. Read the information carefully and apply it to your own finances.

RETHINK THE ROLE THAT MONEY AND SPENDING MONEY PLAY IN YOUR LIFE

Chapter 5 challenged you to figure out why—the *real* reasons and root causes—your credit history got damaged before you began the credit rebuilding process. It reviewed a number of possible reasons, positing among other explanations that maybe financial troubles surfaced because you bought into society's overemphasis on spending money and having a lot of possessions. This section explores that idea in greater detail.

It's easy to develop a "spend, spend, spend" mind-set. Every day, we are bombarded by media messages telling us that if we buy a particular product or service, we'll be happier, have more friends, look better, or have a more rewarding love life. Our celebrity-driven culture encourages us to value people according to what they wear, where they live, and the car they drive. As a result, many consumers feel a lot of pressure to "keep up with the Joneses," and they spend every penny they make and use credit to help them live far beyond their means.

Living that way is dangerous! It's akin to playing with financial fire, because consumers who run up their credit cards and have little or nothing in savings are left with virtually nothing to fall back on if they lose their jobs, have their hours cut, become ill or injured and acquire a lot of expensive medical bills, and so on. Those consumers also risk becoming disconnected from themselves and the world around them—they lose sight of what's really important in life because they are so focused on money and what money can buy.

Having to deal with serious money troubles and to rebuild your credit after those troubles are over offers you an opportunity to step back and take a hard look at your priorities. What have you been doing with your money? What role has money been playing in your life? If you are honest with yourself and if you are truly interested in putting your finances on a more solid footing for now and for the future, this self-analysis can help you lay the groundwork for living a more financially responsible and a more emotionally rewarding life. Let's look at some of the following money-related thinking and behaviors that may have gotten you into trouble:

- **You have a "gotta have it now" attitude.** Rather than saving to buy what you want, you've used credit to instantly gratify your every whim. Credit lets you wear the latest fashions, enjoy the newest electronic gadgets, and drive the hippest cars right away.

- **You live for today.** Sure, you may think about your financial future once in a while, but you're having so much fun living in the here and now that you never get around to planning for what might happen down the road. You may promise yourself that next month you'll put yourself on a budget, pay down your debts, and set up a savings plan, but you never do.

- **You believe that money really can buy happiness.** Reality check! Take a look at the troubled lives of some of Hollywood's wealthiest stars, most successful models, and biggest sports heroes. They can afford everything that money can buy, yet they have substance abuse problems, eating disorders, issues with anger management, and dysfunctional relationships. Do you think they would have those problems if their lives were *really* happy?

> ### 🖐 Red Alert!
> Don't kid yourself. Bad things don't happen to everyone else but you. Sooner or later, you will experience a setback of one sort or another. That's a reality of life. So be prepared.

If any of these money mind-sets apply to you, it's time for a change in attitude. For example, rethink what it means to be wealthy. How much money you have and how much you spend are only two ways to define wealth. Another way to define wealth is in terms of how you live your life and the relationships you have with others. According to this definition, you are wealthy if the following apply to you:

- You enjoy a satisfying relationship with your spouse or partner.

- Your children are happy and well-adjusted.

- You have friends you enjoy on whom you can rely.

- You have good relationships with your parents and siblings.

- You are in good health.

- You enjoy your work and are not constantly stressed out by it.

- You take time to appreciate the beauty around you—a gorgeous sunset, a full moon, the smell of the springtime air just after it's rained, the sound of your child's laugh, and so on.

- You take time to help others who are less fortunate. Volunteering your time is a great way to appreciate what you have, and it helps you keep what you have and don't have in perspective.

- You find peace and meaning in your life through an organized religion, by practicing yoga, meditating, reciting daily prayers, or something else.

Although money can't buy any of the things on the above list, they are keys to a happy, fulfilling life, regardless of how much money you make and how much "stuff" you have. Focusing on them rather than on what your money (and your credit cards) can buy will not only help you appreciate and enjoy your life more, but also will help you keep your priorities straight and avoid financial trouble.

GET HELP CHANGING THE ROLE OF MONEY IN YOUR LIFE

If you have a difficult time examining your money mind-set and changing your relationship with money, or if you want an objective sounding board with whom you can talk, meeting with a mental health professional is a good idea. A therapist can help you step back, figure out why you do what you do when it comes to money and credit, and provide you with the support you may need to change your thought patterns and break bad habits. Resources for finding a mental health professional in your area include the following:

- **A close friend or family member.** If you're not self-conscious talking about your money problem and you know that one of your friends or relatives has worked with a mental health professional, ask him or her for the name and phone number of that professional.

- **Your family doctor.** Your doctor should be able to refer you to a number of qualified mental health professionals.

> **❢ Hot Tip**
>
> You may need to meet with a number of mental health professionals until you find one with whom you feel comfortable. For mental health counseling to truly benefit you, you need to be able to open up about your problem, and that may involve sharing details about your life that may be embarrassing, make you feel very vulnerable, or even cause you to cry. Most mental health professionals will not charge you for an initial "get acquainted" meeting or will charge you less than the cost of a regular office visit.

- **The websites of Mental Health America (MHA) and of the American Mental Health Counselor's Association (AMHCA).** You can search at both of their websites for mental health professionals in your area. Go to *therapist.psychologytoday.com/nmha* to find a professional in the MHA's database and to *www.find-a-counselor.net* to locate a professional near you in the AMHCA's database.

- **Your local or state mental health association.** These associations can also refer you to mental health professionals in your area.

Other possible resources that may also help you include a spiritual advisor or a life coach. A life coach is someone who helps individuals clarify the changes they want to make in life and come up with a plan for achieving these changes, and provides them with support along the way. You'll find countless life coaches on the Internet. Some may also be listed in your local Yellow Pages or in one of your local newspapers or magazines. However there are no national standards for life coaches, so when you are choosing one you'll have to rely on your instincts and judgment about whether a particular coach is right for you.

> ### 🖐 Red Alert!
>
> Although outsiders can provide you with support and understanding when you are trying to change your relationship with money, the hard work is up to you. No one can change your relationship for you..

Another option to consider if you simply can't control your spending is to start attending Debtors Anonymous meetings. You may even want to get a D.A. sponsor—someone who will be available to you on a one-on-one basis to answer your questions, help you understand why you overspend, provide you with advice, share his or her own experiences trying to get control of spending, and give you the support you need to develop a new relationship with money. To learn more about Debtors Anonymous, go to *www.debtorsanonymous.com.*

THE ROAD TO BECOMING SMARTER ABOUT YOUR MONEY

If you're like most consumers, you probably know relatively little about money management. The subject was most likely not covered in your high school or college curricula, and when you were growing up your parents (who may know very little about money management themselves) might not have taught you much about the subject either. However, just as it's never too late to build a stronger, more muscular body by lifting weights, it's never to late to build your financial muscles by getting educated about the basics of money management. The next several sections of this chapter help you get that education by providing need-to-know information about using credit, spending, financial goal setting, and more.

Understanding the Different Types of Credit

The word *credit* is a broad word that's often used to represent a variety of specific kinds of credit. Understanding what sets one type of credit apart from the others helps prepare you to choose the right type when you want to finance a purchase rather than pay for it with cash. The following are three basic types of credit:

1. **Revolving (or installment) open-end credit.** A creditor gives you a set amount of credit—your credit limit—and you can use that credit whenever and however you want, as long as you pay at least the minimum due on your outstanding balance each month. Credit cards are the most common example of this kind of credit.

2. **Revolving closed-end credit.** A creditor gives you a fixed amount of credit for a specific purpose and you are responsible for making regular payments of a certain amount until you've paid off your credit balance. Car loans, mortgages, and student loans are common examples of this type of credit.

3. **Nonrevolving credit.** Although this kind of credit is usually associated with a high credit limit, you don't get to repay whatever you've charged in installments over time. Instead, the full balance is due when you receive your bill. The most common example of this kind of credit is the traditional American Express credit card.

These three different types of credit can be either secured or unsecured. When you are approved for unsecured credit, you simply give your word to the creditor that you will repay the debt. Examples of unsecured credit include most MasterCard and Visa cards, student loans, accounts that you've established with your doctor or with your neighborhood grocer, and retail store charge accounts with business, such as Home Depot or Banana Republic. Also, when you borrow a relatively small amount of money from a bank (less than $1,000), the loan will probably be unsecured; although as you learned in chapter 6, if you have a bad credit history, you may be unable to qualify for even a small unsecured bank loan.

If you are approved for secured credit, on the other hand, you must guarantee that you'll pay your debt by giving the creditor a lien on one of your assets. A lien gives the creditor a legal right to take the asset, known as your *collateral,* if you don't repay the debt according to your credit agreement. For example, if you don't pay your mortgage the lender may take your home, and if you don't pay your car loan you risk having it repossessed. If you pay a secured debt according to your agreement with the creditor, the creditor will release its lien once you've paid the debt in full. At that point, the creditor will no longer have any claim on your collateral.

Ordinarily, the more money you want to borrow, the more likely you will have to collateralize the debt with one of your assets. Also, the worse the state of your finances, the more likely you'll have to secure any credit for which you are approved.

What You Need to Look at When You Shop for Credit

When you're in the market for credit, you'll get the best deal if you compare offers, because some deals are better than others and will cost you less in interest and fees. To thoroughly compare terms you must read all of the details in the fine print of a credit card offer or, in the case of a loan, all of the provisions in the agreement. That's where you'll find most of the really important information about the credit.

The federal *Truth in Lending Act* makes it easier to compare credit offers by requiring that banks, savings and loans,

> **❢ Hot Tip**
>
> When you receive a credit card in the mail, it will come with detailed information about all of the terms of credit associated with the card. Don't throw that information out until you have read it carefully. (You may want to file the information for future reference.) If you throw it out without reading it first, call the creditor's customer service number to ask to that the information be sent to you again. Call the same number if you have a question about the terms of credit associated with a credit card.

and credit card companies provide you with specific up-front information about the terms of the credit they offer to you. Those terms include the following:

- **The annual percentage rate (APR) associated with the credit.** This is the best measure of the true cost of the credit. For a loan, the APR represents the effective annual interest rate on the loan when all points and one-time fees associated with the loan and other costs are taken into account. The APR on a credit card represents the interest rate you will pay on any balance you may maintain from month to month. The lower the APR the better—a high APR can significantly increase the total cost of the credit.

- **Whether the APR is fixed or variable.** If the rate is fixed, generally it will stay the same for a long time (unless your card agreement includes a universal default clause and the clause is triggered). However, even the rate on most fixed-rate cards agreements is apt to increase occasionally. Creditors have the right to adjust a card's APR occasionally for any reason after giving you 15 days advance notice of the change. The interest rate on a variable-rate card, however, may be adjusted every month or every quarter as the rate to which the card is indexed goes up or down. If a card has a variable rate, be sure you understand when the rate can increase, how often it can increase, and whether there is a cap on how much the rate can increase.

❗ Hot Tip

When you are in the market for a credit card, pay attention to all of the APRs associated with the card. For example, a card may have an introductory APR that's a lot lower than the APR that applies after the introductory period is up, and different APRs will apply to purchases, cash advances, and balance transfers. The APRs on some cards will go up or down depending on the amount of your outstanding card balance, and the APRs on other cards will increase if you are more than a certain number of days late with your monthly payment.

- **The periodic interest rate associated with the credit.** This is the interest rate that you'll be charged on an outstanding debt during a particular period of time, usually by the day (periodic daily interest) or by the month (periodic monthly interest).

- **The balance calculation method.** This applies to credit cards and refers to the method that a credit company will use to calculate the outstanding balance on a card. Some methods will cost you a lot more in interest than others. The least expensive methods are the *adjusted balance* and the *average daily balance excluding new purchases* method (the most common method). Avoid the *two-cycle average balance including new purchases method* and the *two-cycle daily balance excluding new purchases* method whenever possible because they are the most expensive.

- **The grace period.** Grace periods, normally associated with credit cards, relate to the amount of time that you will have to pay the total balance owed on a card after the end of the last account billing cycle in order to avoid being charged interest on that balance. Some cards have a grace period as long as 25 days, but most cards have shorter grace periods, and some have no grace period at all. If you anticipate carrying a balance on your credit card, you want as long a grace period as possible. Always avoid no-grace-period cards if at all possible.

- **The fees associated with the credit.** Fees can really increase the cost of using credit, so the fewer the number of fees and the lower the fees the better. Common credit card fees include an annual or membership fee, a late fee, a fee for exceeding your credit limit, a bounced check fee, a fee for transferring a balance, and a cash advance fee. Believe it or not, some cards charge a fee for not using the cards enough! The fees associated with a loan vary somewhat depending on the type of loan but always include a late fee. Other possible types of fees include an application fee, a loan-origination or processing fee, and an appraisal fee.

The Criteria Creditors Consider When You Apply for Credit

When you apply for credit, most creditors will take into account one or more of the following criteria when deciding whether to give you credit you want. They also take these criteria into account when determining the terms of the credit.

🤚 Red Alert!

Beware of credit card agreements that include a *uinversal default* clause. This clause gives a creditor the right to increase the interest rate on your card if you are late paying some other debt, even if you've never been late with any of your payments to that particular creditor. Most unversal default clauses give you at least 30 days notice before an increase will take effect. Unfortunately, universal default clauses are increasingly commonplace.

- **Your character.** Creditors believe that how you've managed credit in the past is a good indicator of how you're likely to handle new credit in the future. To make this assessment, they look at your credit history and/or check out your credit score (usually one or more of your Classic FICO Scores). If they find too much negative information in your credit history or if your credit score is too low, they will either deny you credit, give you less credit than you asked for, and/or give you credit with less attractive terms.

- **Your capacity.** When creditors are trying to assess your ability to repay the credit you've applied for, they may take into account some or all of the following: the amount of your household income, how much debt you already have and the amount of your monthly debt payments, and the value of your assets, among other things. They may also use financial ratios to determine the overall health of your finances. The most common ratios are reviewed later in this chapter.

- **Your collateral.** When you apply for a substantial amount of credit, the creditor will want to know whether you have any assets that you can use to secure or collateralize the debt. If you have a bad credit history or a low credit score, creditors may require that you collateralize even relatively small loans.

The kinds of assets that creditors are looking for when you have to put up collateral include assets like your home, any rental property or undeveloped land you may own, a vehicle, a boat, or the cash in your savings account. If you don't own any of these kinds of assets, if all of your assets are already securing other debts, or if none of your assets are worth enough compared to the amount of credit for which you've applied, your credit application will probably be denied.

MONEY-MANAGEMENT RULES OF THUMB

Once you have established new, positive credit for yourself, it's important to manage your finances responsibly so you avoid damaging your credit history again, qualify for the most attractive terms of credit, and have plenty of money in savings. Therefore, always keep these nine money-management rules of thumb in mind:

1. **Set financial goals, and begin a regular savings program in order to achieve your goals.** Delayed gratification can make the achievement of a goal you've set for yourself that much sweeter. Chapter 5 discusses goal setting.

2. **Avoid overspending, and work toward your financial goals by living on a budget.** Remember, budgeting is not necessarily about sacrifice and deprivation; it's about taking control of your money by planning ahead of time exactly what you will do with it. Chapter 5 explains how to build and live with a budget.

3. **Pay your debts on time.** Late payments damage your credit history and lower your credit score. Also, paying late fees increases the overall cost of your credit.

🖐 Red Alert!

Don't risk damaging your credit record by cosigning for the credit your child, another family member, or a friend can't get on his or her own. If you do, you will be legally responsible for paying the debt you cosigned for if your friend or relative falls behind on the payments or stops making them. Furthermore, if he mismanages the debt you've cosigned for, the negative information associated with the account may end up not only in his credit history, but in yours, too. Bottom line: If you are asked to be a cosigner, say no.

---

4. **Pay with cash whenever possible, but when you use your credit cards, pay off the balances as quickly as you can.** Letting the balances build increases the total cost of your purchases because of interest charges (and maybe late fees, too). Large balances can also lower your FICO scores and make you more vulnerable to serious money troubles if you experience a financial setback.

5. **Whenever you are in the market for credit, comparison shop to get the best deal.** Treat this process just as you would if you were purchasing a new car or appliance. Figure out your best deal using the information in the beginning of this chapter.

6. **Review all three of your credit histories regularly for errors and clear them up using the dispute process outlined in Chapter 3.** Also, stay alert for signs of identity theft. If you believe or know that you are a victim of that crime, follow the instructions in chapter 10 for protecting your credit and preventing the identity thief from further victimizing you.

7. **Use financial ratios to make sure that your spending and debt levels are in line with what is generally acceptable to lenders.** The next section of this chapter reviews the key ratios you should know about.

8. **If you begin to have trouble meeting your financial obligations, review your budget for expenses you can reduce, look for ways to increase your income, and pay high-priority obligations first, like your mortgage, home equity loan, and your car loan.** If you want help figuring out what to do, schedule an appointment right away with a reputable nonprofit credit counselor. Do whatever it takes to avoid damaging your credit history and lowering your credit score. Chapter 9 provides more detailed advice about what to do if you are in financial trouble.

9. **Exercise your legal rights as a consumer.** Consumer laws are there to protect you, so use them! If you need help protecting your rights, get advice and assistance from a consumer law attorney. This book has already educated you about your legal rights under the Fair Credit Reporting Act and the Credit Repair Organizations Act (chapters 1–3 and 5–6, respectively). Later in this chapter, you'll learn about some of your other consumer rights.

If you are married and especially if your relationship is rocky, you should also be aware of the actions you should take during your marriage to minimize the impact of a possible divorce on your post-divorce financial life. Figure 8.1 on page 141 gives you the run down on those actions.

KNOWING HOW MUCH DEBT IS TOO MUCH

Careful money managers avoid owing too much to their creditors. Accumulated debt will damage your credit history and credit score, jeopardize your ability to get new credit with affordable terms, and leave you at greater risk for money troubles. Sometimes, owing money is an inevitable part of money managing. *But how much debt is too much?*

That question can be answered in several ways. One way is to review the following list of questions. The more often you answer yes, the more likely it is that you owe too much to your creditors, which means that you must reduce your spending and/or increase your income:

- Am I using credit and/or credit advances to pay for some of my basic living expenses, like groceries, my phone bill, or utilities because I don't have enough money in my checking account to cover them?

- Have I fallen behind on any of my financial obligations?

- Can I only afford to pay the minimum due on some of my credit cards?

- Are any of my credit cards maxed out?

- Are my creditors sending me notices demanding that I pay up or threatening me with legal action or the loss of any of my assets?

- Are debt collectors calling me?

- Am I transferring balances from one credit card to another to deal with my debt?

- Am I losing sleep, feeling depressed, drinking too much, or fighting with my spouse or partner because of my financial situation?

Another way to answer the question is to apply the very same ratios to your finances that some creditors will apply when they are evaluating your credit application, especially when you want to borrow a substantial amount of money. Financial planners may use the same ratios to help their clients assess the overall health of their finances and to pinpoint areas for improvement. Following is information about the more commonly used financial ratios:

- Your total monthly debt payments, *not including* your monthly mortgage or rent payment, should equal no more than 20 percent of your gross monthly income (your income before taxes and other deductions), but you should shoot for 10 percent.

- Your total monthly debt payments, *including* your monthly housing cost, should be no more than 36 percent of your gross monthly income.

> **▼ Hot Tip**
>
> You should be able to pay off all of your credit cards and other open-end credit over a 12- to 24-month period using no more than 10 percent of your take-home pay.

Don't panic if your percentages are a little higher than these standards. It's possible that housing costs, transportation costs, or some other category of living expense is relatively high in your area compared to most other areas of the country. If any of your ratios are more than a few percentage points higher, however, you have cause for concern.

FIGURE 8.1 Tips for Protecting Your Finances from the Impact of Divorce

Getting a divorce can be one of the most financially devastating events in your life. But you can take steps ahead of time to soften the financial blow should your marriage end. Although planning for the possibility of divorce may be less than romantic, an estimated 50 percent of all marriages end that way—preparing for the worst is unfortunately an example of wise financial planning. Also, planning for divorce prepares you for managing your own finances, should you become widowed.

Your planning should include the following:

■ **Maintaining a solid credit history in your own name.** No law requires you to cancel your individual credit accounts and merge your credit with your spouse's when you say "I do" on your wedding day. In fact, canceling your individual accounts is a bad idea. You'll need a solid-gold credit history in your own name after you divorce (or become widowed) to get new credit, insurance in your own name, employment, and a place to live.

■ **Minimizing the amount of joint credit you share with your spouse.** If you divorce, those joint accounts will get closed, and if you then go to those same creditors and ask them to give you new credit in your own name, you will have to apply for the credit if the joint accounts were based on your spouse's income and credit history. If you have little or no individual credit, your applications may be denied even if you managed your family's finances—including the joint accounts—when you were married.

■ **Staying actively involved in the management of your family's finances and in investing for your future.** Two heads tend to be better than one when it comes to money management. For example, you may be better at certain aspects of money management than your spouse. Or maybe your involvement in the management of your family's finances may mean that you catch potentially costly errors your spouse is about to make, or that you make sure you don't miss important deadlines associated with your debts, taxes, or other financial matters. Also, being involved, you'll be able to manage your family's finances without skipping a beat if your spouse becomes physically or mentally incapacitated. If you do end up going through a divorce, your insider's knowledge of what your family owes and owns can help you ensure that your share of the settlement is financially fair and can help reduce the cost of your divorce because you won't have to hire outside professionals to obtain that information. Finally, after you begin living on your own, you'll be less apt to make expensive mistakes with your money and can begin working toward the future faster.

■ **Keeping your job skills up-to-date if you don't work outside the home so that if your marriage ends, you can earn a living.** Although your divorce agreement may provide you with some spousal support, most likely it will only be temporary and it may not cover all of your living expenses.

LEARNING ABOUT THE CONSUMER LAWS THAT PROTECT YOU

Many consumers develop financial problems, get ripped off, or spend more money than they should because they don't know about the laws that protect them when they apply for credit, use credit, use their debit or ATM cards, or are contacted by debt collectors. In part, this is because our elected officials are a lot better at passing laws than they are at ensuring that every citizen knows about the laws. Also, public schools provide little or no education about consumer laws. The fact is, most consumers will not read a book about consumer law just for the fun of it. Unfortunately, therefore, more often than not consumers don't learn about their consumer rights until after those rights have been trampled on, their finances have been damaged, they've spent money that they shouldn't have, or they've been harmed in some other way.

This book has already educated you about your credit reporting rights under the Fair Credit Reporting Act and Fair and Accurate Credit Transactions Act (see chapter 1) and it's also explained how the Credit Repair Organizations Act protects you when you want help repairing your credit (see chapter 7). This chapter has also explained the various terms of credit that you're entitled to know before you apply for credit according to the Truth in Lending Act. The rest of this chapter will help you broaden your consumer law horizons by educating you about other federal consumer laws you should know and reviewing your options should your legal rights be violated. Chapter 10 provides specific information on your legal rights as a victim of identity theft.

The Equal Credit Opportunity Act (ECOA)

This law protects you when you apply for credit, when you're evaluated for credit, and when a creditor considers your income. It applies to all creditors who regularly extend credit to consumers, including banks and credit unions, credit card companies, finance companies, and retailers. The ECOA says that creditors cannot discourage you from applying for credit because of your gender, marital status, age, race, national origin, or because you receive public assistance income. It also says that creditors cannot ask you about the following:

- Your gender, race, national origin, or religion, or whether you are divorced or widowed.

- Your marital status, assuming that you are applying for individual unsecured credit. However, if you live in Arizona, California, Idaho, Louisiana, Nevada, New Mexico, Texas, or the state of Washington and you apply for individual *secured* credit, creditors can ask you about your marital status.

> ### 🖐 Red Alert!
>
> If you are close to retirement age when you apply for credit, the ECOA allows creditors to consider that fact, as your income will probably go down after you retire, which could affect your ability to repay your debt.

The same is true, no matter what your state of residence, if you apply for joint credit or secured credit.

- Your plans to have children, including your birth control method, or how you intend to raise them—whether you intend to be a stay-at-home parent, for example.

- Your spouse, unless you're applying for joint credit, your spouse will be an authorized user on your credit account, you need your spouse's income to qualify for the credit, or if you live in a community property state. Also, you can be asked about a former spouse who is paying you child and/or spousal support.

The ECOA also says that creditors cannot do the following:

- Ask if you are receiving alimony, child support, or separate maintenance payments, unless they tell you first that you don't have to share this information with them, and assuming you're not relying on those payments to qualify for the credit you've applied for. However, they can ask if you're obligated to pay alimony, child support, or separate maintenance payments.

- Refuse to consider any alimony, child support, or separate maintenance payments you may be receiving, although the creditor can ask you to provide proof that the payments are regular and reliable.

- Consider whether you have a telephone listed in your name. However, they can consider whether you have phone service at your home.

- Take into account the race of the people who are living in the neighborhood where you want to purchase a home when you apply for a mortgage. The same is true when you apply to refinance a mortgage you already have, or when you apply for money to remodel your home.

- Refuse to consider money you may receive through a pension, annuity, retirement plan, or a part-time job. Also, they can't value this income at less than its full amount.

- Discount the total value of your income because of your gender or marital status. In other words, if your employer pays you an annual salary of $60,000, creditors can't consider only $50,000, $55,000, and so on of your income when they evaluate your application.

- Refuse to treat any public assistance payments you may receive like any other income.

The ECOA also gives you the right to do the following:

- Establish credit using your married name, maiden name, or a hyphenated last name that combines your last name and your spouse's last name.

- Get credit without a cosigner, assuming you can qualify for the credit on your own. If you do need a cosigner, the law doesn't require that it be your spouse, unless you live in a community property state and you apply for secured credit, such as a car loan or a mortgage.

- Be told whether your application has been approved or rejected within 30 days of filing a complete application. If your application is denied, you must be given the specific reason for the denial—e.g., your income was too low or you don't have a long enough employment history. Not providing you with a specific reason is illegal. Also, if you are approved for credit but at less favorable terms than you asked for, you're entitled to be told why, if you ask.

- Keep your own credit accounts if your marital status changes, you retire, turn a certain age, or change your name, unless the creditor concludes that you either can't afford to continue paying the accounts or that you're unwilling to continue paying them.

- Have information about an account that you share with your spouse reported to the credit reporting agencies (CRAs) in both of your names.

Fair Credit Billing Act (FCBA)

This law helps you resolve account billing problems when you use an open-end credit account like a MasterCard or a retail store charge card. It covers such problems as the following:

- Charges on your statement that you did not make or authorize
- Mathematical errors
- Payments you made that were never posted to your account
- Credits you were given that are missing from your account, such as credits for merchandise you purchased with your credit card and then later returned
- Statements you missed because they were sent to your old mailing address instead of your current address, assuming you

notified your creditor of the change in your address in writing at least 20 days prior to the end of the account billing period

The FCBA lays out the process you must follow to try to resolve any of these problems, and the process that the creditor must follow once you contact it about the problem. For example, to initiate the protections of the FCBA, you must write the creditor about the problem no later than 60 days after the first account statement containing the error is mailed to you. Attach to your letter copies of any information you may have that helps prove the error in your statement, and then mail the letter to the creditor's address for billing inquiries. Do *not* include your letter in the same envelope that you use to mail your account payment. Model your letter after the one in Figure 8.2.

FIGURE 8.2 Sample Letter Disputing Information in Your Account Billing Statement

[*Date*]
[*Your name*]
[*Your address*]
[*Your account number*]

[*Name of creditor*]
Billing Inquiries
[*Address of creditor*]

Dear Sir or Madam:

   I am writing to dispute a billing error in the amount of $_____on my account. The amount is inaccurate because [*Describe the problem*]. I am requesting that you correct the error, that my account be credited for any finance charges and other charges related to the disputed amount, and that you send me an accurate account statement.

   Enclosed are copies of [*Describe any information you are sending with your letter, such as receipts cancelled checks, and so on*] that support my position. Please investigate this matter and correct the billing error as soon as possible.

Sincerely,
[*Your signature—sign your name as it appears on your account*]

Enclosures: [*List what you are enclosing*]

Once the creditor receives your letter, it must acknowledge its receipt within 30 days, unless the problem has already been resolved. Also, the creditor must resolve the problem within two billing cycles, but in no more than 90 days. If the creditor violates any provision of the FCBA, it is prohibited from collecting the amount of money in dispute or any related finance charges, up to $50, even if your account statement turns out to be accurate.

While the creditor is investigating the problem in your account, you don't have to pay the amount in dispute or any related charges, like finance charges. However, you must pay the rest of your bill. Meanwhile, the creditor can't take any actions to collect the amount you are disputing (or related charges), nor can it restrict your use of the account, close the account, or report to a CRA that the amount in dispute is past due.

If the creditor confirms the error in your billing statement, it must tell you in writing how it intends to correct the error. If the creditor determines that your account statement is accurate, it must immediately convey that information to you and also tell you how much you owe as a result and why. In turn, you're obligated to pay the amount you disputed plus all applicable finance charges. You may also have to pay the minimum due amount that you did not pay during the investigation period.

You can tell the creditor in writing that you disagree with its conclusion and that you won't pay the disputed amount, but you must do so within 10 days of receiving the creditor's notice. At this point, however, the creditor can report the account as past due to the CRAs, although it must also report that you don't believe that you owe the money.

Other Rights Under the FCBA

The FCBA also gives you certain rights when you purchase goods or services with a credit card and the goods or services turn out to be defective, shoddily made, or not what you ordered. However, the law only applies if you made your purchase with a MasterCard, Visa, Discover Card, or an American Express, not with a store-issued credit card. Also, the purchase must amount to at least $50 and must have been made either in your state of residence or within 100 miles of your current billing address. Assuming you try without success to resolve the problem directly with the business that sold you the product or service, the law says you can take the same actions against the business that your state law allows you to take.

The Credit Practices Rule

The Federal Trade Commission's Credit Practices Rule prohibits finance companies, retailers such as auto dealers, furniture stores, and department stores, and credit unions that make loans or that allow consumers to pay for a purchase in installments from including certain provisions in their consumer credit agreements. The rule does not apply to real estate purchases, savings and loans, banks, or to bank cards such as MasterCard or Visa.

The prohibited contract provisions include the following:

- A requirement that if the creditor sues you for not paying your debt, you agree to waive your right to be notified up front about any court hearings related to the lawsuit and that you waive your right to hire an attorney in the lawsuit.

- A requirement that you will forfeit your right under your state's law to hold on to certain assets if you don't pay your debt as agreed, and that the creditor reserves the right to take some of your assets as payment. However, this provision does not apply if the debt is secured—a car loan or a mortgage, for example—because the creditor can take your collateral.

- A clause allowing you to agree in advance to have money automatically taken out of your paychecks and paid to the creditor if you default on your debt. However, it's permissible for you to arrange to have your payments deducted out of your hourly wages or paycheck if you want.

- A requirement that you collateralize a debt with certain household and uniquely personal items of yours that have little value to the creditor but are of significance to you, such as family photos, kitchen appliances, your family bible, family pets, and so on. However, if you borrowed money to purchase any of these items and you used the items as collateral, the creditor can take them (repossess them) if you don't repay your loan.

The Credit Practices Rule also protects you when you agree to cosign someone else's debt. It requires creditors to provide cosigners with a specifically worded notice that clearly warns about the responsibilities you are taking on.

The Fair Debt Collection Practices Act (FDCPA)

The FDCPA gives you certain rights when a debt collector, including an attorney who regularly collects debts for clients, contacts you. The law also prohibits debt collectors from taking certain actions to collect a debt from you. However, the law applies only to debt collectors who work for debt collection agencies, not to debt collectors who are employees of a creditor. The FDCPA says the following about debt collectors:

> **❗ Hot Tip**
>
> The Credit Practices Rule prohibits a creditor from charging you a late fee because you haven't paid a previous late fee. That's called *pyramiding*.

- A debt collector can contact you about a debt that it says you owe via the mail, the telephone, fax, or telegram.

- It cannot call you at work if the debt collector knows that your employer doesn't want you contacted there.

- It must tell you in writing how much you owe, the name of the creditor to whom you owe the money, and what action you should take if you don't agree that you owe it within five days of contacting you for the first time about the debt.

- It cannot contact you before 8 A.M. and after 9 P.M., unless you say it's okay.

- It is prohibited from trying to collect more than the amount of the debt, unless your state's law allows it.

- It cannot try to trick you into accepting a collect call or paying for a telegram sent to you. Also, the debt collector cannot contact you using a postcard or an envelope that indicates it came from a debt collector.

The law also prohibits a debt collector from the following:

- Using profane language

- Calling you repeatedly

- Threatening to harm you or your property in some way

- Implying that by not paying the debt you are committing a crime or that you'll be arrested

- Implying that she is a police officer, attorney, or government official, or works for a CRA when that isn't true

- Misrepresenting the amount of money that you owe or telling you that papers she has sent or will send to you are legal documents if they are not

- Telling you that the debt collector will seize some of your assets, put a lien on some of your assets, sell some of your assets, or sue you, unless the debt collector (or the creditor that she is working for) really intends to take one or more of those actions and is legally entitled to do so

The debt collector *can* contact your friends, neighbors, or relatives to find out where you live, where you work, and your phone number in order to help it collect a debt from you. However, she cannot tell any of them why she is trying to contact you.

What to Do If a Debt Collector Contacts You

If a debt collector contacts you, the FDCPA offers you several different ways to respond:

- **Request written verification of the debt.** Even if you know that you owe a debt, asking for written proof buys you time to figure out what to do about it. Also, if you're not sure that you owe the debt or that the amount of the debt is accurate, you may request written verification.

- **Dispute the fact that you owe the debt or dispute the amount of the debt.** You must put your dispute in writing within 30 days of the debt collector's first notice of the amount of money it intends to collect. After receiving your letter, the debt collector must either provide written proof that you owe the money or stop trying to collect on the debt. While pulling the proof together, the debt collector must report the debt as "in dispute" whenever it sends information about it to a CRA. Meanwhile, the debt collector can't contact you again other than to confirm receipt of your letter or to provide you with the proof you requested, and it must suspend all efforts to collect from you.

- **Tell the debt collector not to contact you again.** Although taking this step won't make the debt go away, it's a good move if a debt collector is being difficult to deal with. It's also a good option when you can't afford to pay a debt that you owe and you don't want the debt collector to continue contacting you about it. On receipt of your letter, the debt collector must stop communicating with you, other than to confirm the receipt of your letter or to let you know about any steps it is about to take to collect the debt—for example, if the debt collector intends to sue you.

- **Acknowledge the debt and pay it in full, or work out a way to pay it over time.** Another option is to try to get the debt collector to agree to let you settle the debt for less and report to the CRAs that you *paid as agreed.*

> 🖐 **Red Alert!**
>
> Never pay a debt that you owe if doing so will make it difficult or impossible for you to pay your essential living expenses and your most important financial obligations, like your child support, mortgage, and car loan.

The Electronic Fund Transfer Act (EFTA)

The EFTA protects you when you use your debit or ATM card, bank online, schedule automatic debits to your account (as well as automatic deposits and transfers of money out of your bank account that you authorize over the phone), and make other electronic fund transactions involving your account. It also gives you certain rights if you lose your ATM or debit card, or if either card or your PIN number is stolen from you.

If you discover an error related to a transaction that is covered by the EFTA, write or call your bank within 60 days of the date that the first statement containing the error was mailed to you. If you call, the bank may direct you to send a letter within 10 business days. Your letter should clearly explain the error, including the dollar amount and why you believe the amount is wrong, and should indicate what action you want the bank to take. Be sure to indicate the date of the error and your account number, and when you sign the letter, use the same name as the one that's on the account. Attach to the letter a copy of your bank statement with the error highlighted.

> 🖐 **Red Alert!**
>
> If you wait longer than 60 days to contact the bank about a problem in your bank account, the bank is not legally obligated to investigate the problem.

Your bank must begin an investigation into the error within 10 days of receiving your letter, must complete the investigation within 45 days—although there are a few exceptions to this requirement—and must notify you in writing of its conclusion. If it confirmed the error, your bank must correct the problem within one business day.

It's important to act as soon as you discover that your ATM card, debit card, or PIN number is lost or stolen, because the sooner you report it to your bank, the more you are protected. For example, if you report the loss or theft within two business days of discovering it, your loss is limited to $50, but if you wait longer, the law says that your loss can be as much as $500. Also, if you don't report an unauthorized transfer of funds out of your account within 60 days of the date that the statement reflecting the transfer is mailed to you, your potential loss is unlimited.

WHAT TO DO IF YOU BELIEVE YOUR CONSUMER LEGAL RIGHTS HAVE BEEN VIOLATED

The first thing to do if you think that your legal rights have been violated is to contact the business involved and give it an opportunity to correct the problem. Whatever it did or didn't do may have been an innocent mistake. Put your concerns in a polite letter. In the letter, explain your problem, cite the law that you believe the business has violated, and indicate what you want the business to do to resolve the matter. If you already tried to resolve your problem by phone, note in your letter the date of each conversation along with the name and title of the person you spoke with. Be sure to include your daytime contact information in the letter so that the business can get in touch with you if necessary, and attach to the letter copies of any information you may have that helps prove the problem you are writing about or that helps document your previous efforts to resolve the problem. If you don't hear from the business within the reasonable amount of time—seven to ten business days—follow up with a phone call.

If the business you write to doesn't respond to your letter or fails to take appropriate action to resolve your problem, you have several options. If your problem does not involve a lot of money and/or if not resolving it won't have a significant negative impact on your life or your credit history, you may want to simply move on. Otherwise, it's time to get help from a consumer law attorney. Examples of serious violations include the following:

> **❗Hot Tip**
>
> Whenever your legal rights have been violated, send all letters related to the violation via certified mail with a return receipt requested, and make copies of the letters before you send them. Never send original copies of any documents you have that help prove the violation of your rights, and maintain a detailed record of whatever steps you take to try to resolve your problem

- You are wrongfully denied important credit.

- You are unable to get damaging information removed from your credit history.

- A debt collector is harassing you day and night.

- A creditor and/or a CRA has failed to take appropriate action in response to information you provided about the theft of your identity.

Complain to the Appropriate Government Agency

When you write your letter, send a copy of it to the appropriate federal government agency charged with enforcing the law that you believe the business has violated, together with copies of any supporting documents you may have. If your state also has a law that applies to your problem, do the same with the state agency charged with enforcing that law. Put the letters "CC" (stands for "courtesy copy" or "carbon copy") at the very bottom of the letter (below your signature) that you send to the business that has violated your rights and then list the agency(ies) to whom you are sending the copies. Doing so may put extra pressure on the business that has violated your rights to resolve your problem, because it wants to avoid trouble with the enforcement agencies.

FIGURE 8.3 Federal Agencies to Contact When Your Consumer Rights Have Been Violated

When you believe that your consumer rights have been violated, file a written complaint with the appropriate federal agency. The list below tells you which agency to contact based on the type of business that violated your rights.

TYPE OF BUSINESS	WHO TO CONTACT
CRAs and any creditors not listed below	Federal Trade Commission Consumer Response Center Washington, DC 20508 1-877-382-4357
National banks (The word *national* or the initials *NA* will appear after the name of the bank.)	Office of the Comptroller of the Currency Compliance Management Mail Stop 6-6 washington, DC 20219 1-800-613-6743
Banks that are members of the Federal Reserve System (except for national banks)	Federal Reserve Board Division of Consumer & Community Affairs Washington, DC 20551 1-202-452-3693
Savings and loans and federally chartered savings banks (These banks will have the word *federal* or the initials *FSB* in their names.)	Office of Thrift Supervision Consumer Complaints Washington, DC 20552 1-800-842-6929
Federal credit union (The banking institution will have these three words in its name.)	National Credit Union Administration 1775 Duke Street Alexandria, VA 22314 1-703-511119-4600
Banks that are state-chartered and that are not members of the Federal Reserve System	Federal Deposit Insurance Corporation consumer Response Center 245 Grand Avenue, 64108-2638 Kansas City, MO 64108-2638 1-877-275-3342

The agency to contact depends on the nature of the violation and the particular type of organization that violated your rights. Figure 8.3 lists the various federal agencies that enforce consumer laws and the types of businesses they regulate. If you're unsure which agency to contact, call the FTC or a consumer law attorney. If your state has a law that also applies to your legal problem, contact your state attorney general's office to find out which state agency should receive a copy of your letter, as well.

Finding an Attorney

There are a number of resources for finding a consumer law attorney who can help you resolve your legal problem. Those resources include the following:

- **Your local or state bar association.** Most bar associations offer an online attorney referral service. You may also be able to get a referral by calling your state or local bar association.

- **Friends or relatives** who may have hired a consumer law attorney in the past and were pleased with the help their attorneys provided.

- **A lawyer you may know.** The attorney will probably know which consumers law attorneys in your area have good reputations and handle problems like yours.

- **The National Consumer Law Center.** Visit *www.consumerlaw. org* or call 1-617-523-8089.

- **The National Association of Consumer Advocates.** Visit *www. naca.net* or call 1-202-452-1989.

- **An attorney-located website.** There are many of these sites, including Lawyers.com, Martindale.com, and Attorney.com. In addition to offering basic information about various legal topics, the sites allow you to search for an attorney by city and by area of the law. However, many of these sites require that attorneys pay a fee to be included in their database, so the fact that an attorney is listed on a site says nothing about the attorney's experience or abilities.

When you use one of these resources, be clear about the exact nature of your particular problem. Some consumer law attorneys are more knowledgeable than others about particular areas of consumer law, and it's always best to work with an attorney who has specific experience resolving a problem like yours.

It's a good idea to schedule an initial consultation with any attorneys you may be thinking about hiring. Most attorneys won't charge you for this meeting. The following are some of the questions to ask at the meeting to help you determine if the attorney is right for you:

- Have you handled cases like mine in the past and what outcomes did you achieve?

- How would you approach my problem?

- If I hire your firm, will you actually work on my case or will you turn it over to one of your associates?

- If I hire your firm, what should I expect?

- How do you charge for your services? (If you have a strong case, most attorneys will probably agree to take your case *on contingency*. Chapter 1 explains how contingency fees work.)

- About how long do you think it will take to resolve my legal problem one way or another?

> **▼ Hot Tip**
>
> If you can't find an attorney willing to help you on a contingent fee basis, contact the legal aid or legal services office in your area if your income is low or moderate. An attorney with one of these offices may handle your case for little or no money. However, these offices do not handle all types of legal problems. Even if they can't help you, they may be able to suggest a resource in your area that can.

Avoid attorneys who don't seem interested in your problem. For example, they don't ask you questions, they don't seem to be listening to you, or they don't look at you while you are speaking. Also, steer clear of attorneys who don't give you complete answers to your questions or just talk to you in legalese.

Planning Your Lawsuit

After evaluating the details of your case, your attorney will decide how much to sue for and whether to sue in federal or state court. If your state has a law that's similar to the federal law that applies to your problem, the attorney may sue in state court because your state law may allow you to sue for more money. State courts tend to be less crowded than federal courts, which means that your case will be heard sooner. Also, lawsuits in state courts tend to be less expensive.

If you win your lawsuit, you may be awarded *damages* to compensate you for the financial harm that the business inflicted by violating your rights.

> **❗Hot Tip**
>
> Depending on the nature and the seriousness of your problem and the amount of money involved, the attorneys you meet with may suggest that you file your own lawsuit in small claims court. This is a do-it-yourself court for legal matters that involve relatively small amounts of money—no more than $5,000 to $15,000, depending on your state. The procedures and processes are more consumer-friendly than in other types of courts and court personnel can help answer your questions.

Damages might include any income you lost, your out-of-pocket expenses, interest and fees you should not have had to pay, and so on. Also, the business may be required to take certain actions. For example, a CRA may be required to remove certain negative but true information from your credit history. The court may also award you a certain amount of money in punitive damages. Punitive damages are intended to discourage a business from breaking the law again, and to warn other similar businesses not to break the law. The court may also direct the business to pay all of your court costs and attorney fees.

We all know that nothing is certain in life, so even if you apply all of the information in this chapter, you may experience a financial setback. Therefore, the next chapter offers you "just-in-case" information—information that can help you minimize the impact of a setback on your credit histories and credit scores. It also warns you about various money-making "opportunities" that will make your situation worse, not better, and about things you should never do when you're trying to turn your finances around, like writing bad checks and continuing to use credit.

Minimizing Damage to Your Credit When You're Having Money Problems

9

There are no guarantees in life, and that's certainly true when it comes to your personal finances. As hard as you may try to mange your money responsibly and make wise decisions, when it comes to managing your money and using credit, events beyond your control—like an expensive illness, an unexpected job loss, or having to buy a new car because your old one died—can play havoc with your finances. As a result, you may begin having problems covering your living expenses and paying all of your debts.

If you find yourself in this situation, it's critical that you do everything you can to avoid serious damage to your credit histories and to your FICO scores. That includes acknowledging what has happened, figuring out the likely impact on your finances, and making appropriate adjustments to your credit and your lifestyle. This chapter helps you understand the importance of these steps and reviews your options. After a short discussion of why acknowledging what's happened to your finances (or what you anticipate happening) sooner rather than later is critical, the chapter goes on to review the various actions you can take in response, starting with the actions that are relatively easy to take on your own and progressing to options that are more complicated to pursue.

The chapter also warns you about business scams that may sound tempting if you are looking for a way to increase your income. In addition, it advises you about actions you should never take when you're having money problems.

STEP 1: ACKNOWLEDGE THE PROBLEM

To effectively deal with a change in your finances, you must recognize that the change has occurred. The sooner you do, the more options you'll have, and the less impact the change is likely to have on your credit histories and credit scores.

> **! Hot Tip**
>
> If you know ahead of time that you need to replace your vehicle, or your job is about to end, or your child is going to have surgery and your insurance will only pay a small fraction of the total cost, or that some other change is about to impact your financial life, start planning for the change right away. That may include spending less, making more, and building up your savings account.

In fact, if you recognize what has happened right away and make the appropriate adjustments, your credit histories and credit scores may not be affected at all. However, if the change is serious and will have a serious negative effect on your finances, don't wait too long to respond to what has happened. Your credit accounts may be turned over to debt collectors, your secured creditors may threaten to take your collateral, your unsecured creditors may sue you, and you may be forced to file for bankruptcy. Each of these consequences obviously will be very damaging to your credit histories and credit scores.

One of the very best ways to be aware of signs of financial trouble is to use a budget to plan and monitor your spending. Although it's not the only way to assess the state of your finances, it's an easy-to-use, no-cost monthly barometer of your financial health. Chapter 5 explains how to set up and use a budget.

STEP 2: TIGHTEN YOUR BELT

Spending less may be all it takes for you to weather a financial setback with little if any damage to your credit history. Therefore, review your budget to identify expenses you can reduce or eliminate. Focus first on your variable expenses, like the amount you have budgeted for things like eating out, going to the movies, and for body-care products and services. You tend to have the most control over those types of expenses, and generally they're not essential to your life. Although you may not want to cut back, doing so is a small price to pay if it means that you can pay all of your living expenses and keep up with your debts. Also, once your financial situation has improved, you may be able to add back into your budget some of the spending you cut out.

If you need help figuring out where to cut back, set up an appointment with a counselor at a reputable credit counseling agency. The counselor's services will be free or low cost, depending on your finances. Chapter 7 provides detailed advice and information for finding a good credit counseling agency.

STEP 3: INCREASE YOUR INCOME

Besides reducing your spending, you may also need to increase your income. If that's the case in your situation, begin thinking about what you can do to increase your household income as quickly as possible. (If you have a spouse or partner, he or she should do the same.) The following are some options to consider:

- Work more hours at your current job.

- Get a second job. You may be able to work in the evenings or on weekends.

- Do freelance work. If you'll be doing the same kind of work as a freelancer that you do in your current job, make certain that you didn't sign an agreement with your employer that prohibits you from working for your own or outside clients.

- If your spouse or partner works at home taking care of your young children, consider whether it makes financial sense for him or her to get a paying job. Take into account how much income he could earn versus how much it will cost to work outside the home, taking into account expenses like childcare, transportation, and parking. If it will cost more to work outside the home than he can earn, it won't be a sensible move.

■ Find a new, better paying job. Unfortunately, finding a more lucrative job won't happen overnight. It will probably take you at least a few months. Therefore, although it may be a long-term answer to your financial problems, it's not a quick fix for most people.

✋ Red Alert!

If your spouse or partner can generate more money than it will cost him or her to work outside the home, but the amount of the additional money will be quite small, getting a paying job may not make sense because employment will almost certainly disrupt your family's established routines. This would add stress to your life—something you may not need more of right now if your financial problems are already making you feel stressed out. Too much stress may make it difficult for you to concentrate at work, interfere with your sleep, and make it harder for you to make good decisions.

Watch Out for Business Scams!

When you are exploring possible options for increasing your household income, be wary of ads for business "opportunities," like stuffing envelopes or processing medical claims. Typically, these ads emphasize the amount of money you can make "in your free time" and how quickly you can make it. More often than not, these kinds of opportunities are scams.

You may learn about these types of opportunities through ads in your local newspaper or by reading a flier that's left on your car windshield or posted on the bulletin board at your local grocery store. Some business "opportunities" are promoted through TV infomercials. An infomercial is a 30-minute or hour-long paid advertisement that is produced to appear as though it's regular TV programming. Infomercials commonly air on weekend mornings or late nights, and they often feature everyday people who claim that they've made millions of dollars in their free time by flipping real estate (investing in a piece of real estate, maybe making some improvements to the property, and then selling it as soon as possible), investing in the stock market, and so on. Regardless of the type of opportunity, more often than not, in order to take advantage of it you'll have to purchase software, a directory, supplies, a training manual, business leads, or something else from the business promoter. None of these supplies will be cheap and most will be useless.

Federal law requires any business opportunity promoter who charges more than $500 for the chance to work with it to provide you with written information about how much you can earn, along with the percentage of consumers who have pursued the same opportunity recently and how much they all earned. However, even if it costs less than $500 to invest in an opportunity that you find attractive, ask for this information in writing anyway. In addition, ask the business promoter to provide the following information in writing, too:

- Its legal name and address

- The number to call if you have questions

- A detailed description of the business opportunity

- A detailed description of the kinds of support and assistance the promoter will provide to you

- The total cost of the business opportunity

- All terms and conditions related to your payment by the promoter, if the business opportunity involves you providing the promoter with specific products or services

If a business opportunity promoter refuses to provide this information to you or if it only wants to provide it to you by phone, it's safe to assume that whatever it's trying to sell you is a scam. Don't bite!

Sell Stuff That You Don't Need

If cutting your budget and/or earning more income don't help you meet all of your financial obligations, consider selling some of your belongings. You probably have lots of things that you don't use anymore and that are just taking up space, like clothes your children have outgrown, furniture, books, and toys that are gathering dust in your attic, equipment and supplies for a hobby you gave up that are stored in your basement closet, the exercise equipment you never use, and so on. Although these items may not be worth much to you anymore, they may be valuable to someone else. Selling your old stuff may not make you a bundle of money, but it could generate enough cash to pay some bills.

Depending on what you are selling and how much time and effort you want to devote to finding buyers for your items, you may want to use one or more of the following resources to sell your stuff:

> **▼ Hot Tip**
>
> One person's trash is another person's treasure, so never assume that what you have is not marketable. You may be surprised to discover just how much people are willing to pay for your cast-off items, especially if they are in good condition. Vintage items and collectibles are especially popular.

> **▼ Hot Tip**
>
> If you don't have the time to sell your own items on eBay and then ship them to the buyers, an eBay *trading assistant* may be just what you need. Use eBay's *Trading Assistant Directory* to locate the trading assistants who may work in your area. Trading assistants get paid by taking their fee out of the sale proceeds.

- **Craigslist** (*www.craigslist.org*). List your items for free on this no-frills Web site. It's the first place many consumers think of when they are in the market for a specific item, especially offbeat or unusual items.

- **eBay** (*www.ebay.com*). Let people from all over the world know about the items you are selling by listing them on eBay. For an overview of the eBay selling process, go to *www.microsoft.com/athome/moredone/sellonebay.mspx*. Plenty of books also provide tips and advice for getting the most for your items on eBay.

- **Place an ad in the classified advertising section of your local newspaper.** This is a good option if the market for what you are selling is primarily local. Most larger newspapers post classified ads on their websites and also include them in their print editions.

Having a garage or yard sale is another way to sell the items you don't need anymore. Organizing and working at a garage sale can be time-consuming and tiring, but people with a lot of good items to sell have been known to make a couple thousand dollars during a one-day sale. If you decide to have a garage sale, get the word out using posters, yard signs, and newspaper advertising, and by posting the sale on garage sale websites. Also, don't forget to let your friends and coworkers know about your sale.

> ❗ **Hot Tip**
>
> The Yard Sale Queen offers lots of savvy advice at *www.yardsalequeen.com* about how to have a successful yard sale.

You should also consider selling more valuable property that you can do without, like a car that you don't really need, an RV, a boat, a motorcycle, and so on. However, if you still owe money on any of these assets and any of them sell for less than the full amount of your outstanding loan balances, you won't be able to complete the sale until you pay the balances in full.

> ❗ **Hot Tip**
>
> When you sell something like a car, an RV, or a boat, you not only eliminate any monthly payments you may be making on loans associated with those items, but you also eliminate the cost of insuring them, operating and maintaining them, and so on.

STEP 4: CONTACT YOUR CREDITORS

Depending on your financial situation, reducing your spending, selling assets, and making more money may not be enough to allow you to cover all of your monthly expenses. In that case, you may want to find out if your creditors are willing to change your debt payment obligations on a temporary or permanent basis.

🖐 Red Alert!

If you wait months to get in touch with your creditors and meanwhile you're falling farther and farther behind on your payments to them, your creditors are going to be less inclined to work with you. This isn't to say that contacting your creditors as soon as you realize that you're having financial problems is a guarantee that all of them will give you what you ask for, but you have a better shot at hearing your creditors say yes when you contact them sooner rather than later.

Doing Your Homework before You Call

Before you contact your creditors, some up-front planning and analysis are in order. For example, you should figure out which creditors to contact first, because some of your debts are more important than others—the consequences of what may happen to you if you fall too far behind are greater with some than others. Also, using your budget as a guide, you should decide how much you can afford to pay on your debts each month and therefore, what concessions you need from each creditor to be able to keep up with your financial obligations.

To begin this analysis, create a list of all of your of debts. Next to each debt, note the name of the creditor, whether the debt is secured or unsecured, the amount that you're currently obligated to pay on the debt each month, and the interest rate on the debt. Figure 9.1 provides a sample worksheet for recording this information.

Use this sheet or create one like it to organize your debt information before you contact your creditors to ask for changes in how you must pay the debts.

FIGURE 9.1 Debt Analysis Worksheet

For each of the below, list:

Name of Creditor/Amount of Outstanding Debt/Monthly Payment/
Secured or Unsecured/Interest Rate

Secured Debts

_____

_____

Priority Unsecured Debts

_____

_____

_____

Other Unsecured Debts

_____

_____

_____

_____

_____

Next, review your budget so you know exactly how much money you can realistically afford to pay to each of your creditors and what concessions to ask them for. For example, you may want to ask them to lower your monthly payments by a certain amount on a temporary or permanent basis, let you make interest-only payments for a time, or lower your interest rate. Consider your secured debts first, because if you fall too far behind on them you may lose the collateral that secures the debts. For example, your mortgage lender may take back your home or your auto lender may repossess your vehicle. However, you should also treat certain types of unsecured debts as top priorities given the serious consequences of not paying them. Those debts include the following:

> ### 🖐 Red Alert!
>
> If you owe at least $1,000 in past-due child support, your state's child support enforcement agency is required to report that fact to each of the credit reporting agencies.

- **Past-due rent.** You risk eviction if you fall too far behind on your rent. The eviction will damage your credit histories and most landlords will be reluctant to rent to you.

- **Utilities.** If you lose your utility service, you'll have to pay what you owe in order to get the service restored and you'll probably have to pay the provider a substantial deposit.

- **Court-ordered child support.** If you ignore your obligation to help support your kids, you risk having the state that issued the court order take some of your assets to pay what you owe, put a lien on your bank account, or even take the money in your account, cancel your driver's license, or take your state or federal income tax refund, among other possible actions.

- **Past-due federal taxes.** If you ignore your obligation to Uncle Sam, you risk having your paychecks garnished (a certain percentage of your income will be deducted from each paycheck and sent to the IRS until your tax debt is past off).

- **Past-due federal student loans.** When you don't keep up with your student loan payments, the loan may be turned over to a debt collector, your wages may be garnished, and you won't be entitled to any additional federal student aid, among other possible consequences.

Except for the unsecured debts on the previous list, address your unsecured debts last. Depending on the state of your finances, you may not have enough money to pay all or any of them, and the consequences of not paying most unsecured debt—like credit card debt—are usually less serious than not paying secured debts or priority unsecured debts. This is not to say that you shouldn't live up to *all* of your financial obligations, but sometimes that's simply not possible.

You may face the following consequences if you fall too far behind on most unsecured debts:

> **! Hot Tip**
>
> When you contact a creditor, it's a good strategy to ask for a bigger concession than you really need, because the creditor may want to do a little bargaining. Asking for more gives you some room to negotiate. However, don't start off a conversation with a creditor by asking for so much that the creditor won't even consider working with you. Be reasonable.

> **! Hot Tip**
>
> Some creditors will agree to let you settle your debt by paying less than the full amount that you owe on it. Ordinarily, however, they won't agree unless your account is at least 120 days past due and they've concluded that it's unlikely that they will ever collect the full amount of your debt.

- The debts may be turned over to collections.

- Some of your unsecured creditors may sue you for the money if the amounts that you owe to them are substantial. If they win their lawsuits, they may get permission from the court to put liens on some of your assets, which would mean that you wouldn't be able to borrow against those assets or sell them or transfer them without paying off the creditors first.

> ## 🖐 Red Alert!
>
> Some of your creditors may not agree to give you what you want unless you agree to do something in return. For example, they may insist that you get a cosigner, or when the debts are secured, they may require that you increase the amount of your collateral.

- The creditors may write off your debts as uncollectible. Sometime later, however, if your financial situation improves, they may try again to collect from you.

If you want help figuring out how much you can afford to pay your creditors or if you want help negotiating with them, get in touch with a reputable nonprofit credit counseling agency. Chapter 7 tells you how to find a good one. The agency may suggest that you participate in a debt management plan. If you agree, the credit counseling agency will figure out how much you can realistically afford to pay your creditors each month over a three- to five-year period, and then will contact your creditors on your behalf to try to get them to agree to those amounts.

Whenever You and a Creditor Reach an Agreement

If you and one of your creditors reach an agreement, ask the creditor to put the terms of the agreement in writing. It should spell out exactly what you and the creditor agreed to, including all applicable dollar amounts, interest rates, due dates, fees that may apply, and the duration of the agreement. It should also spell out under what circumstances you and the creditor will be considered to have defaulted on the agreement, and the consequences of a default. If the creditor refuses to memorialize the terms of your agreement in writing, prepare your own agreement. Then sign the agreement and send a copy to the creditor. Be sure to revise your budget so that it reflects the terms of your agreement.

> ## 🖐 Red Alert!
>
> Credit counseling agencies only include unsecured debts in debt management plans. If you need help negotiating your secured debts, get in touch with a consumer law attorney.

CONSOLIDATE YOUR DEBTS

Debt consolidation is another option when you cannot afford to pay your essential living expenses and all of your debts. It involves paying off existing debt using new, lower interest debt in order to reduce the total amount of money that you have to pay to your creditors each month. Some examples of ways to consolidate debt follow:

- Transfer your credit card debts to a different card with a lower interest rate.

- Pay off debt by getting a debt consolidation loan.

- Borrow against the equity in your home through a home equity loan or a home equity line of credit in order to pay off debt. Your equity is the difference between its market value and the total amount that you owe on it. For example, if your home is worth $250,000 and you owe $100,000 on it, your equity is $150,000.

- Refinance your home and borrow more than you need to pay off your current mortgage. Use the extra money to pay off debt.

> **Hot Tip**
>
> When you consolidate debt, you reduce the number of payments you have to make to your creditors each month. The benefit? With fewer creditors to pay each month, you are less likely to miss a payment and thus less likely to increase the total amount that you owe because of late fees and interest charges.

- Borrow against the cash value of your life insurance policy, assuming it's a whole life and not a term policy.

- Get a loan from your 401(k) retirement plan.

Although debt consolidation can be a good way to reduce the total amount of your monthly financial obligations, it's not a panacea. If you are a habitual overspender or if you have poor money-management skills, it's possible that once you take some of the financial pressure off by consolidating, you could turn around and take on too much debt again. Also, there are potential drawbacks associated with each debt consolidation option, such as the following:

> ## ✋ Red Alert!
>
> Be careful about trading unsecured debt for secured debt. The risk you take is that if you fall behind on your secured debt payments, you may lose your collateral.

- If you transfer credit card debt to a card with a low-but-temporary interest rate—unless you can pay off the new debt before the low rate—ends you may find yourself paying a higher rate on the new debt than the rates you were paying on the debts you consolidated.

- When you borrow against the equity in your home, or refinance and take cash out to consolidate your debt, you risk losing your home if you can't keep up with the payments on the new debt. If you borrow against the equity in your home, borrow as little as possible and focus on paying off the debt as fast as you can. That way, you'll help reduce the likelihood that you'll lose your home.

- If you don't repay the loan that you get from your life insurance policy, you could create a financial hardship for your spouse or partner after your death if he or she needs 100 percent of the policy death benefit to pay living expenses as a widow. When you consolidate debt by borrowing against your life insurance policy, you don't have to repay the loan according to a fixed schedule. In fact you don't have to repay it at all. However, if you're not disciplined about repaying the loan, upon your death the insurance company will deduct your outstanding loan balance from your policy proceeds before cutting your beneficiary a check.

- Unless you repay any money that you borrow from your 401(k) plan within five years, and assuming you were younger than 59 and a half when you got the loan, you'll be charged a 10 percent penalty on the unpaid balance *and* you'll be taxed on that balance for federal income tax purposes as though it's earned income. Ouch!

🖐 Red Alert!

■ Some home equity lenders have a hidden motive. They want you to default on your loan so they can take it. Predatory home equity lenders may encourage you to borrow more money than you asked for initially or more than you feel comfortable borrowing; they may arrange to have your home appraised for more than it's worth so you can borrow more money than you could otherwise; they may ask you to sign a loan agreement before you've agreed on all of the terms of your loan; or they may ask you to sign a loan agreement even though it doesn't spell out all of the terms on which you agreed.

■ Don't consolidate debt by trading a fixed-rate mortgage for a variable-rate mortgage. Initially, your mortgage payments on the new loan will be lower, but gradually the rate may begin to creep up, and depending on how high it goes, your mortgage payments may be higher than they were before you consolidated—maybe far more than you can afford. You face a similar risk if you consolidate a fixed-rate mortgage with an interest-only mortgage, because unless you can pay off the balance on the new mortgage before the interest-only period ends once you have to begin paying both principal and interest on the loan you may be paying a lot more than you were on the mortgage you paid off.

FILE FOR BANKRUPTCY

If your finances are in dire shape because you owe too much to your creditors relative to your income, your only real option may be to file for bankruptcy. Although this will be devastating for your credit histories and will cause your credit scores to plummet, if your creditors are about to take some of your assets (like your home or your car) you really have no other choice but to file.

Depending on the specifics of your financial situation, you'll either file a Chapter 13 reorganization bankruptcy or a Chapter 7 liquidation bankruptcy. As soon as you file, the court will issue an automatic stay, which requires your creditors—with a few exceptions—to stop trying to collect their money from you while you are in bankruptcy.

🖐 Red Alert!

Most creditors look more kindly on consumers who try to pay as many of their debts as possible through a Chapter 13 bankruptcy. Although the *Fair Credit Reporting Act* allows credit reporting agencies to report consumer bankruptcies for 10 years, all three of them report Chapter 13 bankruptcies for just seven years.

A Chapter 13 bankruptcy may help you reduce the amounts that you owe on some types of debts and will give you between three and five years to get caught up on your past-due debts by paying them according to a debt reorganization plan. Your bankruptcy attorney will prepare this plan for you and file it with the court. The plan shows exactly what you intend to do about each of your debts while you are in bankruptcy. If there are no objections, the court will approve it. When your plan is approved, the automatic stay will remain in effect as long as you live up to the terms of the plan. If you don't, the court will dismiss your bankruptcy and you'll be fair game for your creditors again.

A Chapter 7 bankruptcy wipes out most but not all debts. For example, it doesn't eliminate a federal income tax debt unless the debt is more than three years old when you file for bankruptcy, nor does it get rid of any past-due child support or past-due federal student loan payments you may owe. If you file a Chapter 7, your bankruptcy will last for about six months.

❗ Hot Tip

When you're having serious money troubles, it's a good idea to meet with a bankruptcy attorney as soon as possible, even if you're not sure that you need to file for bankruptcy. The attorney can not only suggest actions that may help you avoid having to file, but can also advise you about actions you should or shouldn't take during the months immediately prior to filing, to help you ensure that you benefit as much as possible from bankruptcy.

It used to be that you and your attorney decided what kind of bankruptcy you would file. However, a recent amendment to the federal bankruptcy law has taken that decision away from you in an effort to force as many consumers as possible into a Chapter 13 bankruptcy. Now, to qualify for a Chapter 7, your finances must pass a federally required means test that takes into account your income and your expenses.

The bankruptcy process is extremely complicated, so never try to file your own bankruptcy. You risk making mistakes that could cost you money and you will not benefit fully from filing. Always work with a bankruptcy attorney.

ACTIONS YOU SHOULD NEVER TAKE WHEN YOUR FINANCES ARE GOING DOWNHILL

Besides understanding the various options that may help you turn your finances around when you're having money troubles, it's also important to be aware of actions you should avoid taking because they could make your financial situation worse. For example, when you're having money troubles, even if they're not serious yet, you should do none of the following:

- **Continue to use credit.** Regardless of whether you are experiencing a temporary cash shortfall or you're having more serious and long-term money troubles, avoid using credit until you are out of the financial woods.

- **Ignore your most important debts.** For reasons this chapter has already explained, it's dangerous to ignore your secured debts and certain types of unsecured debts. When you can't pay everything, pay those debts first.

🤚 Red Alert!

Most car loan agreements let lenders repossess your vehicle if you are just one day late with a payment. Also, in most states, lenders are not required to give you any advance notice. In other words, one day your car is in your driveway and the next day it's gone.

- **Write checks that you can't cover.** If the checks bounce and you can't make good on them, you could be arrested and prosecuted for passing bad checks.

- **Make a promise to a creditor that you can't keep.** If you are feeling a lot of pressure from a creditor about a past-due debt or if you feel guilty about being unable to pay what you owe, you may promise to pay more than you can really afford to pay on the debt or make some other promise related to the debt that isn't realistic. When you can't live up to your promise, the creditor is more apt to turn your debt over to collections or take some other serious action to collect what you owe, like sue you or take your collateral.

- **Pay unsecured debt at the expense of secured debt.** Generally, even if your unsecured creditors are extremely aggressive in their demands that you pay what you owe, you should never pay them at the expense of your secured debts. The only exceptions are past-due, past-due student loans, child support and past-due taxes.

- **Get a risky loan.** Some finance companies, for-profit credit counseling agencies, credit fix-it firms, and other types of companies are in the business of preying on financially naïve and uniformed consumers. Among other things, they promote loans that sound great on the surface but usually come with very high interest rates and require that you use your car or your home as loan collateral. Often, the information that describes the terms and conditions of their loans is purposefully vague and confusing.

- **Work with a disreputable credit counseling agency.** Be sure that it's a reputable nonprofit with a proven track record of helping consumers deal with their debts. Chapter 7 discusses how to find a good credit counseling agency.

As you learned in this chapter, no matter how responsible you are with your money, it's possible that a problem that you never anticipated, like an unexpected a job loss or a serious illness, may create financial problems in your life and threaten to ruin the new credit histories you've worked so hard to build. You now should be well-equipped to handle bad financial times should they come your way.

The next and final chapter in this book addresses another subject that, unfortunately, every consumer needs to become educated about—identity theft. This crime can ruin the finances of even the most responsible money manager. Chapter 10 explains how identity thieves work, how to avoid becoming one of their victims, and what to do if your identity is stolen.

The Dangers of Identity Theft

10

Every year, millions of Americans are affected by the crime of identity theft. Identity theft happens when someone steals your personal and/or financial information and either sells it to someone else or uses it for his own benefit. For example, an identity thief may steal your credit card account numbers in order to charge purchases in your name, steal your bank account numbers, and/or debit card and personal identification number (PIN) to take the money in your accounts, use your name to open new credit and bank accounts, establish utility services, rent a place to live, or obtain a driver's license, steal your Social Security number, or file fraudulent tax returns in your name, among other things.

The actions of an identity thief can ruin your finances and cost you a bundle of money, and undoing the damage can take weeks, months, or even years in some instances. A national study released in 2006 by the national research firm Javelin Strategy & Research and the Better Business Bureau indicated that in 2005, nine million consumers were victims of identity theft, and the crime cost each victim approximately $6,383. A recent Federal Trade Commission (FTC) study indicated that, on average, identity theft victims spend 175 hours and $5,000 trying to resolve the problems created by the theft of their identity.

181

The FTC attributed most of this time and cost to the fact that it takes an average of 12 months before consumers realize that they've been victimized. During those 12 months, an identity thief can do a lot of damage to their lives.

There is no 100 percent foolproof way to avoid becoming a victim of identity theft—you don't have total control over who has your information and what is done with it. For example, many businesses, government agencies, and other organizations have information about you stored in paper and computer files, but the files may not be adequately secured. Also, information about you and millions of other consumers has become a valuable commodity that businesses buy, sell, and share with one another without your knowledge or permission. Computerized databases that are easily accessed via the Internet are also a gold mine of information about consumers. Although all this may seem out of your hands, you can take steps to help minimize the likelihood that you will become an identity theft victim, as well as take actions if you are victimized to limit the impact of the crime. This chapter tells you about those steps and actions, educates you about your legal rights with regards to identity theft, and also explains how identity thieves operate.

✋ **Red Alert!**

Most identity theft victims never find out who victimized them. However, according to surveys conducted by the FTC and Javelin Strategy & Research, half of those who do find out who victimized them claim that it was a family member, a friend, a neighbor, or an in-home employee.

HOW IDENTITY THEFT HAPPENS

Identity thieves may use any number of methods to steal your personal and financial information. The following are some of the most common methods:

- **Dumpster diving.** Thieves will rummage through your trash/recycling looking for credit card and bank statements, tax-related information, or anything with your personal information on it. They may do the same at your place of employment or at public dump sites.

- **Phishing.** Thieves will send you fake emails or pop-up messages that direct you to respond via email or to share specific information about yourself at a website. The messages may appear to warn you of a problem with one of your credit accounts, that your account privileges are about to be suspended, or that your account information needs to be updated. The sender may pose as your bank, one of your credit card companies, your brokerage account, a website at which you recently made an online purchase, and so on.

🤚 Red Alert!

Federal law requires any business—including consumer reporting agencies, lenders, employers, landlords, government agencies, mortgage brokers, and automobile dealers, as well as government agencies—to dispose of all paperwork and documents containing information that can be found in your credit file in a way that will minimize the likelihood that an identity thief will read or reconstruct that information. However, the law doesn't spell out specific acceptable disposal methods. Also, there is no real way for the federal government to enforce this requirement.

- **Changing your address.** Identity thieves may divert your account billing statements to a different location that they control by completing a "change of address" form. If you are busy and don't pay close attention to when those statements should arrive, it may be several months before you realize that they never showed up, giving the identity thieves ample time to do major damage to your finances.

- **Skimming.** Some identity thieves who work at restaurants or retail establishments may use a special handheld storage device to record your name and account number when they process your credit card payment. Later, the thief downloads the information from the device onto his or her own computer.

- **Ordering your credit files under false pretenses.** Identity thieves may illegally claim to a credit reporting agency (CRA) that they are an employer, an insurance company, or someone else who is legally entitled to look at your credit file.

■ **Stealing your information the "old-fashioned" way.** Identity thieves may take your purse or wallet, steal your mail, or take information out of your car, such as pre-approved offers for credit, tax records, an insurance policy, your credit cards, and bank statements. Other identity thieves may eavesdrop on a conversation during which you share information about yourself and your finances, lurk close by when you use an ATM so they can see which buttons you push when you enter your PIN number, or even use binoculars or video cameras to capture those numbers.

🖐 Red Alert!

Some identity thieves operate in the workplace. Yes, one of your coworkers may be an identity thief. The thief may remove information from the purse or wallet you've left on your desk or in an unlocked desk drawer, or take the account payments you've left at the receptionist's desk for the mailman to pick up. Other identity thieves may access your employer's personnel records if the records are not well protected.

THE FEDERAL LAWS THAT APPLY TO IDENTITY THEFT

In 1998, Congress made identity theft a federal crime by passing the *Identity Theft and Assumption Deterrence Act* (ITADA). As a result, the Secret Service, the Federal Bureau of Investigation, and other law enforcement agencies are charged with combating the crime. Anyone who is convicted of identity theft faces up to 15 years in prison and fines as high as $250,000. The thief may also have to pay restitution to victim or victims.

Also, with the passage of the *Fair and Accurate Credit Transactions Act* (FACTA), victims of identity theft, as well as anyone who thinks she may be a victim but doesn't know for sure, now have specific rights and protections when it comes to their credit record information, including the right to add fraud alerts to their credit files. Later in this chapter, you will learn about the different kinds of fraud alerts, as well as how to add them to your credit files.

The FTC acts as a clearinghouse for complaints by consumers who are having problems resolving identity theft-related problems when they are dealing with the CRAs or with creditors. It's also responsible for providing victims of identity theft with referrals to possible sources of assistance and with other general information that can help them deal with the crime.

> **▼ Hot Tip**
>
> Some states have their own identity theft laws. Those laws may give you more protections than the federal laws. Go to *www.idtheftcenter.org/statefedlaws.shtml* to find out if your state has such a law. You can also find out about the consumer rights and protections the law provides.

HOW IDENTITY THEFT CAN TURN YOUR LIFE UPSIDE DOWN

Once an identity thief has stolen your personal and/or financial information the thief may use that information to do the following:

- Run up the balances on your credit accounts.

- Open new credit card accounts in your name, run up the balances, and then default on the accounts.

- Open bank accounts in your name and write bad checks on the accounts, or steal some of the checks you have for your existing account. As a result, retail establishments may refuse to accept your checks, because a computerized bad check registry shows that you've been passing bad checks. Worst-case scenario: you could even be arrested for the bad checks!

- Drain your bank account by authorizing electronic transfers in your name or by counterfeiting checks, credit cards, or debit cards.

- Get a car loan in your name. If the car is repossessed, the repossession will show up in your credit files.

- Obtain a mortgage in your name and then lose the home in a foreclosure. The foreclosure will ruin your credit histories.

The identity thief may also do the following in your name:

- Obtain a driver's license with his picture on it

- Establish phone or wireless service, utility service, cable service, and so on

- Rent an apartment. (If the identity thief is subsequently evicted, the eviction will show up in your credit files.)

- File for bankruptcy

- Get a job

- File fraudulent tax returns

It's even possible that an identity thief who is arrested for a crime will give the police your name and then not show up in court. As a result, a warrant for your arrest will be issued and you could be hauled off to jail. What a nightmare!

PROTECTING YOURSELF FROM IDENTITY THIEVES

It takes constant vigilance to protect yourself from identity theft. Letting your guard down just once may be all it takes for an identity thief to victimize you. The following are the most important things you can do to protect yourself from that crime:

- Review regularly all three of your credit reports, looking for accounts you don't recognize or charges that you do not remember making. You may also want to consider subscribing to a credit monitoring service. Chapter 2 discusses the pros and cons of this option.

- *Shred*—don't just toss into the trash—bank records, account statements, pre-approved credit offers, insurance information, old tax returns, and any other documents and records you no longer need that contain your personal or financial information. Crosscut shredders are best.

🖐 Red Alert!

If you subscribe to a credit report monitoring service, don't assume that you've got all of your bases covered when it comes to detecting signs of possible identity theft. You still need to be alert, because the service you use may miss something important in one of your credit histories, and because some signs of identity theft may not show up in your credit history right away or won't show up at all. Some examples a service might not catch: if an identity thief gets a driver's license in your name, sells some of the investments in your brokerage account, gets a job in your name, gives the police your name when arrested, and so on.

- Never leave your wallet, purse, checkbook, credit card billing statements, bank statements, or deposit receipts—*anything* containing your personal information—in your car, even if you lock it.

! Hot Tip

Although businesses and organizations may ask for your Social Security number, only a few—including some government agencies (such as welfare departments and the IRS) creditors, banks, brokerage firms, and employers—can actually require that you share that number with them. Therefore, if any other kind of business or organization asks for your Social Security number, explain that you are not legally obligated to provide it and that you are happy to offer a different identification number instead.

- Don't carry your bank PINs in your purse, wallet, or checkbook. Memorize them instead.

- Never write your Social Security or driver's license numbers on your checks or have those numbers printed on your checks.

- When you are talking on the phone with someone, don't share your personal or financial information with the other person unless you initiated the call or you are absolutely sure that you know with whom who you are speaking. The same advice applies to sharing information via email, at a website, or through the mail.

- Avoid having your mail delivered to a mailbox that's not lockable, or use a post office box.

- If you pay your bills by mail and your mailbox is not lockable, take the bills to the post office rather than leaving them in your mailbox. Better yet, pay your bills online or have the payments automatically deducted from your bank account.

- Only carry one or two credit cards or a debit card with you when you leave the house. Store the rest of your cards in a safe place.

- Review your bank statements, credit card statements, phone bills, and other bills as soon as they arrive, looking for signs of possible fraud, such as charges and withdrawals you didn't make.

- Never open an unsolicited email or click on links in an unsolicited email unless you are sure that you know who sent it and that the sender is reputable. To be absolutely sure, call the business or organization that's supposed to have sent the email to confirm that it did.

■ Review your annual *Social Security Earnings and Benefits Estimate Statements* to make sure that your earnings are accurate. (Every year, every adult who is at least 25 years of age and who been employed and paid into the Social Security System should receive this statement in the mail about three months prior to each of their birthdays.) If your reported earnings seem too high or too low, someone besides you may be using your Social Security number. Call the Social Security Administration immediately at 1-800-269-0271. If your statement never arrives, call the Social Security Administration at 1-800-772-1213.

■ Protect your home computer by using firewalls, anti-spyware, and anti-virus software. Also, update the software regularly.

■ When you choose passwords for your debit card, bank accounts, brokerage accounts, and so on, avoid using your birth date, your mother's maiden name, the last four digits of your Social Security number, and other obvious passwords. Use passwords that combine numbers and letters.

■ Store your personal and financial information in a safe place like a home safe or a lockbox, especially if you live with roommates, are having work done at your home, or if you employ cleaning people, babysitters, and the like.

■ Put a security freeze on your credit reports, if your state has a security freeze law. A freeze locks up your credit record information, and the only way that someone can look at it is with your permission. You may have to pay a fee to a CRA to freeze your credit file— as much as $20 depending on your state—although some states waive the fee if you're adding a freeze because

> **❗ Hot Tip**
>
> The website OnGuardOnline.gov, a joint project of the federal government and the technology industry, provides detailed information about how to protect yourself from Internet fraud and how to secure the information on your computer.

> **❗ Hot Tip**
>
> Prepare for the possible loss or theft of your credit, ATM, and debit cards by creating a record of the cards and storing it in a safe place. Your record should include the name of each card issuer and the numbers to call if one of your cards is lost or stolen, as well as each account number. You can create this record by writing down all of the information on a piece of paper or by laying your cards on a photocopier, making a copy, and then copying the reverse side of the cards.

AFTER YOU FINALLY HAVE IT: PROTECTING YOUR CREDIT

your identity has been stolen. Also, some states won't let you establish a freeze unless your identity has been stolen recently. At the time this book was written, 26 states had freeze laws of some type. To find out if your state is one, go to *www.consumersunion.org/campaigns//learn_more/ 003484indiv.html*. This site also provides details about each state law, as well as detailed state-by-state instructions for freezing credit files.

■ Discuss financial matters on a landline, not on your cell or cordless phone, because it's relatively easy for wireless signals to be intercepted. Also, avoid discussing financial matters on a cell phone when you are in a public place—you never know who is listening.

■ When you are getting rid of a computer, erase all the information on it using a utility wipe program, especially if you do your banking and pay your bills online. If you just delete the information on your computer, a savvy identity thief can access it.

■ Take advantage of all opportunities to opt out of having your personal and financial information shared with others. Also, opt out of receiving pre-approved offers of credit and insurance and receiving other unsolicited offers that may come to you by mail, email, or via the phone. The less often your personal information is used, the less likely that it will fall into the hands of an identity thief.

Identity theft insurance

Identity theft insurance won't help you avoid becoming an identity theft victim, but it can soften the impact of the crime on your pocketbook. Some homeowners' and renters' insurance policies automatically include identity theft coverage or let you pay extra to add the coverage to your policy. Other insurance companies sell identity theft coverage as stand-alone insurance.

On average, a theft insurance policy will cost you between $25 and $50 for $15,000 to $25,000 worth of coverage. The specifics of the coverage vary from company to company and by type of policy, but typically you will be reimbursed for the cost of restoring your identity and of repairing your credit histories, including the cost of any long-distance phone calls you may have to make, as well as the money you may spend on notaries, copying, certified mail, lost wages, and so on.

Take Advantage of Opt-Out Offers

One way to exercise some control over what's done with your personal data is to take advantage of each and every opportunity to opt out of having it bought, sold, or shared. Here's how to do that:

- Call 1-888-567-8688 or go to *www.optoutprescreen.com* in order to opt out of being included on the lists that all three of the CRAs create for creditors and insurers so that the companies can send prescreened offers of credit and insurance to consumers. You may find at least one of these offers whenever you pick up your mail. You can opt out for five years, or you can complete special paperwork to be permanently opted out. However, after you opt out, it may take as long as 60 days before you stop receiving prescreened offers, and you may continue receiving prescreened offers related to any joint accounts you share with your spouse or partner, unless he or she opts out as well. Also, opting out with the CRAs won't stop offers that are not the result of prescreening, such as offers from local merchants and businesses with which you already have a relationship. You will have to contact each of those businesses individually to put an end to them.

- Stop most telemarketing calls by registering your home and cell phone numbers with the FTC's national *Do Not Call Registry*. To do that, call 1-888-382-1222 or go to *www.donotcall.gov*. Your registration will last for five years. Within about a month after signing up, the number of calls you receive from telemarketers should drop off significantly, although you may continue to receive calls from political organizations, charities, and companies conducting surveys, as well as calls from companies with whom you already have an existing relationship.

> **❢ Hot Tip**
>
> Some states have their own do-not-call registries. Contact your state attorney general's office to find out if your state is among them. If it is, enroll in that registry too.

- Minimize the number of national marketers that contact you by mail and via email by adding your name to the Direct Marketing Association (DMA)'s mail and email preference lists. To add your name to the DMA's mail preference list, go to *www.dmaconsumers.org/cgi/offmailing* and complete the online registration form, or print off the form, fill

> **❗ Hot Tip**
>
> Some states have passed financial privacy laws that are tougher than the federal law. Contact your state attorney general's office or your state banking commission or department to find out if your state has such a law, and if it does, how you can use it to protect your privacy.

it out, and return it to: Mail Preference Service, PO Box 282, Carmel, NY 10512. To add your name to the DMA's email preference list, visit *www.dmaconsumers.org/consumers/optoutform_emps*. The cost of opting out with the DMA is $1 per list. If you register online, you must pay the fee with a credit card; otherwise, you can pay with a check or money order. By the way, once you add your name to the DMA's email preference list, you may continue to receive unsolicited emails from businesses that are not members of the DMA, as well as from businesses who are members but who choose to ignore the fact that you have opted out.

■ Opt out of having the banks, credit card companies, insurance companies, and investment firms that you already do business with share or sell your information to others. The federal *Financial Services Modernization Act* (FSMA), also known as the *Financial Modernization and Privacy Act*, requires covered businesses to mail you annual notices that inform you of your right to opt out and that provide you with specific instructions for how to opt out. (If you normally do business with these companies online, the law allows them to contact you via email about your opt-out rights.) To opt out, you may be instructed to call a toll-free number, complete a form online, or mail back a form provided by the business. Follow to the letter the instructions in the business' notices. If you don't, you may not get opted out.

Beware, there are some big loopholes in the FSMA. For example, the law does not allow you to opt out with third-party outside companies that provide a service to your bank such as account servicing or check printing, or with third-party outside companies that have entered into joint-marketing agreements with your bank, credit card company, insurance company, or investment firm to sell their services or products through the mail or by phone. (You can help close this particular loophole by opting out with the FTC and the DMA.) Also, the

FSMA allows banks, credit card companies, insurance companies, and investment firms that are affiliated under a single corporate umbrella to share your personal information with one another and to market to you, if they have had a preexisting relationship with you within the previous 18 months.

Whenever possible, opt out with companies that are in the business of selling or sharing information about consumers, including names, addresses, phone numbers, arrest records, information about any foreclosures and/or repossessions in their histories, and so on. You can learn the names of these data brokers by going to *www.privacyrights.org/ar/infobrokers.htm* at the website of the Privacy Rights Clearinghouse.

KNOWING THE SIGNS OF IDENTITY THEFT

Knowing the signs of identity theft will help you recognize that something may be amiss before the identity thief has had an opportunity to do serious damage to your finances and credit histories. The telltale signs of identity theft include the following:

- Your credit reports include information for accounts you don't recognize or show that you are over your limits on some of your credit cards when you know you haven't exceeded your limits.

- Your credit card account statements reflect charges you don't recognize, or you receive statements for accounts you did not open.

- One of your credit cards is cancelled even though last time you looked there was no outstanding balance on the account.

- Credit cards that you didn't apply for arrive in the mail.

- You're denied credit even though you have an excellent credit history (or at least you thought you did!).

- Your bank statement shows withdrawals you didn't make or checks you didn't write.

- You receive phone calls or letters about merchandise or services you didn't order.

- You receive a demanding call or letter from a creditor about a debt that you didn't pay, but you know you didn't incur the debt.

- Debt collectors start calling you.

- Retailers refuse to accept your checks.

WHAT TO DO IF YOU THINK THAT YOUR IDENTITY HAS BEEN STOLEN

If you believe that your identity has been stolen, take the following actions immediately. Each action is discussed in greater detail later in this chapter:

- Create a detailed record of all incidents of identity theft and of every step you take to resolve the identity theft. Keep copies of all letters you send about the crime and all letters and notices you may receive.

- Add fraud alerts to your credit files.

- Contact creditors associated with the theft of your identity to close existing accounts affected by the identity theft and new accounts opened by the thief, and to dispute all fraudulent charges and withdrawals associated with the accounts. Also, ask the creditor to provide you with written verification that it has complied with your request.

- Get in touch with your bank if the identity thief wrote checks from your bank account or withdrew funds from the account.

🤚 **Red Alert!**

Do *not* agree to pay any fraudulent charges that are the result of identity theft or to cover any checks the identity thief may have written in your name. If a business pressures you to do so, contact a consumer law attorney.

Do the same if the thief opened new bank accounts in your name. Also, clear up any problems related to fraudulent electronic transactions conducted by the identity thief.

■ Dispute all fraudulent information in your credit files. Also, ask each of the CRAs to block the fraudulent information.

■ Tell debt collectors who contact you about debts that an identity thief ran up in your name, that the debts are fraudulent, and that you don't want to be contacted about them again.

■ File a police report with your local police department or with the department in the community where the crime occurred. You may need the report to resolve some of problems that the identity thief may have created in your financial life.

■ Take steps to resolve all other incidents of identity theft.

You should also obtain copies of any applications an identity thief may have filled out in your name, as well as copies of all transactions the thief conducted in your name. You must request this information in writing, and the business you contact is obligated to send you what you've asked for within 30 days of receiving from you all of the information it needs to process your request. Be sure to take advantage of this right, because the records you obtain can be invaluable to ensuring that the identity thief doesn't do additional damage to your finances and could even help law enforcement track down the thief.

Before you mail your request to the business, call its fraud or security department to determine what it will accept as proof of your identity, and the address to which you should send your letter. Also, clarify exactly what additional information the business may need from you to process your request. For example, it may want you to provide it with a copy of the crime report that you filed with law enforcement when you reported the theft of your identity, a completed copy of the FTC's *ID Theft Affidavit* (which is available at *www.ftc.gov/bcp/edu/microsites/idtheft/consumers/index.html*)or it may require you to complete its own affidavit. Commission attorneys, creditors, and consumer advocates created the *ID Theft Affidavit* to make it easier for consumers to prove that they are identity theft victims.

Create a Paper Trail by Keeping Detailed Records

Whenever you are the victim of identity theft, document the impact of the identity theft on your life and the efforts you take to deal with it. Your record keeping may be helpful if you have difficulty exercising your identity theft rights and if you run into problems undoing the damage that the crime inflicts on your credit history and your finances.

Your records should include, among other things, the following:

- Copies of all letters you send and forms you fill out related to the identity theft

- All correspondence and notices you receive about the theft

- All certified mail receipts

- Copies of the credit histories that reflect the identity theft

- Copies of all bills and statements that reflect the identity theft

- Copies of all applications completed by the identity thief and of all paperwork related to transactions the thief conducts

- A record of every phone call you make or receive related to the theft, including the date of each conversation, the name and the title of the person you speak with, and what was said, as well as each person's phone number and email address, if applicable

- All of the money you spend as a result of the identity theft, including the amount of each expense and exactly what it was for, to whom you paid the money, and the date of the expense

- The amount of unpaid time you may have taken off from work to deal with the identity theft, including the date you took off and the number of hours of work you missed

Whenever you contact a business or a government agency by phone to make a request related to the theft of your identity, protect yourself by restating your request in a letter. If the business or agency made any promises to you during your conversation, include them in your letter, too. Also, whenever a business or government organization agrees to take a particular action related to the identity theft, ask that it send you written confirmation that it actually did what it promised. If you don't receive the confirmation, keep asking for it. Don't give up! It's important that you know exactly what has or hasn't been done. Keep all this information in your files.

Finally, whenever you mail a letter related to an identity theft incident, send it certified mail with a return receipt requested so that you know that the letter was received, the date that it was received, and who signed for it. Make copies for your files of all correspondence and other information you are sending.

Add Fraud Alerts to Your Credit Files

When you're a victim of identity theft or believe that you may be, FACTA entitles you to add fraud alerts to your credit files. Once the alerts are in place, whenever an application for new or additional credit is made in your name, or changes are requested to an account you already have (such as a request that a new card be issued for one of

> **! Hot Tip**
>
> Because fraud alerts can slow the approval process when you apply for new or additional credit, provide your cell phone number or your daytime number when you establish an alert so that the creditor can reach you quickly.

your accounts or that the credit limit on an account be increased), the creditor must use "reasonable policies and procedures" to confirm that you submitted the application or made the request, not someone pretending to be you.

You can add free fraud alerts to all three of your credit files by contacting just one of the CRAs. The CRA you contact will pass on your information to the other two. (The same is true if you want to remove the alerts.) The following is fraud alert contact information for each CRA.

- **Equifax**. Call 1-888-766-0008.

- **Experian.** Call 1-888-397-3742 or go to *www.experian.com/identity_fraud/ victim_assistance.html*

- **TransUnion.** Call 1-800-680-7829 or go to *www.transunion.com/corporate/ personal/fraudIdentityTheft.page*

🖐 Red Alert!

The toll-free numbers set up by each of the CRAs to accept reports of identity theft and requests for fraud alerts are automated. In other words, when you call those numbers, you won't speak to a human being. Therefore, speak slowly and clearly so that your information will be recorded accurately. If you have any questions about the alerts, you can call each of the CRAs to speak with a fraud advisor once the fraud alerts are established.

After you've requested that fraud alerts be added to your credit files, order copies of each of your credit histories to verify that the alerts are there.

Depending on your circumstances, you may be entitled to establish one or more of the following types of alerts, each of which lasts for a specific time and gives you specific rights:

- **Initial alert.** You can establish an initial alert whenever you know or suspect that your identity has been stolen. An initial alert will last for 90 days and entitles you to one free copy of each of your credit reports, assuming you request them before the alerts have expired.

- **Active duty alert.** If you're in the military and you are deployed, you can add an active duty alert to your credit files instead of an initial alert. An active duty alert will stay in your credit files for one year and can be renewed if your deployment lasts longer than one year. Also, your name will be removed from the CRAs' marketing lists for prescreened offers of credit and insurance for two years.

- **Extended alert.** This kind of alert remains in your credit files for seven years and entitles you to two free copies of each of your credit reports during the first 12 months that the alerts are in place. Also, during the first five of the seven years, the CRAs cannot include you on any prescreened lists they may develop for credit and insurance companies. To establish an extended alert, you must provide the CRA that you contact with a copy

> **❗ Hot Tip**
>
> You are entitled to designate a *personal representative* who can establish active duty alerts in your name, because doing so may be difficult if you are deployed.

of your *identity theft report*—the form that you filed with your local police department, your state police, or with some other federal law enforcement agency to report the crime. You must also provide the CRA with proof of your identity and any additional information it may require in order to set up the alert. Contact the CRA or visit its website to confirm exactly what information you must provide.

Handle Identity Theft Problems Related to Your Existing Credit Accounts

As soon as you realize that an identity thief has used one of your credit accounts, call the creditor's fraud or security office. Ask that the account be closed and that you not be held responsible for any of the fraudulent charges. Then immediately make the same request in writing. The fed-

> **❗ Hot Tip**
>
> When you are the victim of identity theft, establish an initial or active duty alert right away, as doing either is quick and easy. Then set up the extended alert.

eral *Fair Credit Billing Act* (FCBA) says that your financial liability for unauthorized charges made to your existing credit accounts is limited to $50 if you contact the creditor *in writing* within 60 days of receiving the first statement containing the fraudulent charges.

Before you mail your letter, clarify the address to which it should be sent. *Do not* send the letter to the same address that you use when you pay your account. Model your letter after the one in Figure 10.2. Chapter 8 provides additional need-to-know details about your FCBA rights and responsibilities.

FIGURE 10.2 Sample Letter to Dispute Fraudulent Charges to Your Credit Accounts

[*Date*]
[*Your Name*]
[*Your Address*]
[*Your Account Number*]

[*Name of Creditor*]
Billing Inquiries
[*Creditor's Address*]

To Whom It May Concern:

I am writing to dispute the following fraudulent charges to my account. They are the result of identity theft.

* [*Create a bulleted list of the fraudulent charges*]

I am requesting that each of the above charges and any related finance charges or fees be removed from my account and that the outstanding balance on the account be adjusted accordingly.

I have enclosed copies of [*Describe whatever you are enclosing that helps prove the theft of your identity, such as a copy of the FTC ID Theft Affidavit you may have completed, a copy of the police report, and so on*] to help prove the fraud.

Please investigate this matter, remove the fraudulent charges from my account, and credit my account accordingly.

Sincerely,
[*Your name—sign your name as it appears on your account*]

Enclosures: [*List what you are enclosing*]

Resolve Problems with New Credit Accounts Opened by an Identity Thief

If an identity thief has opened a new account in your name, contact the creditor's fraud or security department to explain what has happened. Ask that the account be closed immediately, and find out what information you must provide the creditor in order to dispute the fraudulent charges that the identity thief made in your name.

Identity Theft Problems Related to Bank Accounts, Checks, and ATM and Debit Cards

If the identity thief used your bank account or opened a new bank account in your name, contact the security or fraud department at the bank to explain what has happened, and ask that the account be closed immediately. If the identity thief wrote outstanding checks on your existing accounts either by stealing your checks or counterfeiting checks, ask the bank to put stop payments on the checks and to report its actions to whatever check verification service the bank uses, so that businesses will know not to accept the checks. Also, contact your state's department of banking or banking commission to find out if your state has a law that limits your liability for losses in the case of forged or stolen checks and fraudulent electronic drafts. (No federal law does so.) You can find contact information for the banking department or commission in your state at the website of the Conference of Bank Supervisors (*www.csbs.org*), or you can find the phone number in the Blue Pages of your local phone book.

When an identity thief writes bad checks in your name, it's also a good idea to contact each of the national check verification companies to ask them to add a security alert to the information they maintain on you and to ask them to tell retailers not to accept any checks written on the fraudulent accounts. Chapter 1 provides contact information for the major check verification companies.

If an identity thief has stolen your ATM or debit card, or the account number associated with such a card, cancel the card immediately. According to the federal Electronic Fund Transfer Act (EFTA), if you report the loss or theft of your ATM or debt card within two days of realizing that you no longer have the card, you are only liable for up to $50 in fraudulent transactions. If you wait between three and 60 days to report the loss or theft, you can be held liable for up to

> **❗ Hot Tip**
>
> Some ATM and debit cards offer more protections than others when the cards or the card account numbers are stolen. Read your card agreement to learn exactly what your rights are.

$500—and if you wait longer than 60 days, your liability for any fraudulent transactions conducted by the identity thief after the 60 days may be unlimited. However, both MasterCard and Visa will hold consumers responsible for only $50 worth of fraudulent transactions regardless of when they report the loss of theft of their ATM or debit cards. Chapter 8 provides more information about the EFTA.

Dispute All Fraudulent Credit Record Information and Get the Information Blocked

In addition to adding fraud alerts to your credit files—and putting freezes on each of the files if your state has a security freeze law—review each of your credit histories as soon as possible, so that you can be sure that you haven't overlooked a fraudulent account or fraudulent charges on one of your existing accounts. Then, take the following steps immediately.

- Dispute all fraudulent credit record information with the CRA that is reporting it. Dispute it with the provider of that information, too.

- Ask each of the CRAs to block the fraudulent information. Make this request even if you've already disputed the information and added fraud alerts to your credit files. When you write a letter to a CRA to request a block, explain that your credit file contains information that's the result of identity theft, and that you want that information blocked. Spell out exactly what information you want blocked. Also, highlight the information on the copy of your credit history that you received from the CRA and attach it to your letter. In addition, be sure to include with your letter proof of your identity and whatever proof of the identity theft the CRA requires.

> **❗ Hot Tip**
>
> An information provider cannot continue reporting fraudulent information to the CRAs once you've provided it with all of the information it needs to confirm that the information is the result of identity theft. However, if it later determines or learns that the information is *not* the result of identity theft, the information provider can begin reporting it again.

Once the CRA has received all of the information it requires, it must establish the block within four business days, and it must let the provider of the blocked information know what it has done. At that point, the provider can no longer report that information to any of the CRAs. Also, the information provider cannot turn the debt over to a debt collector or sell it to a debt collector.

> ### ✋ Red Alert!
>
> A CRA can deny your request for a block or rescind a block that's already been established if it believes that the information you want blocked is not the result of identity theft or that you acquired goods or services as a result of the information you want blocked.

Respond to Debt Collectors That Contact You About Fraudulent Debts

If you are contacted by debt collectors about unpaid fraudulent debts that are in your name, let them know that the debts are not yours and are the result of identity theft. Then follow up with a letter to that effect. If the debt collectors continue to contact you about paying the debts, put an end to their phone calls and letters by exercising your rights under the federal *Fair Debt Collection Practices Act* (FDCPA). Chapter 8 provides detailed information about your FDCPA rights.

In the meantime, contact the creditors to whom the debt collectors say that you owe the debts and follow the advice earlier in this chapter about handling the fraudulent charges. If any of your creditors sold the fraudulent debts to the debt collectors, then you'll have to contact them directly to prove that the debts don't belong to you.

Report the Crime to Law Enforcement

As soon as you know that your identity has been stolen, file a crime report about the theft with your local police or with the police in the community where you believe the theft occurred. Review the report before it is finalized to make sure all of the information related to the crime is accurate and that every incident of identity theft that you know about is included in the report. If any incidents are missing, ask that they be added.

Get a copy of the final report and put it with the rest of the information in your identity theft file. Also, write down the name and phone number of the police investigator you worked with in case you need it later. If the investigator refuses to give you a copy of the report, ask to speak with his superior. If you are unable to get a copy, write down the report number.

Some police departments are not very helpful to victims of identity theft and are reluctant to let identity theft victims file police reports. If you have a problem filing a report, be persistent and don't take no for an answer. Also, check with your state attorney general's office to find out if the department is required to let you file a report. If your state does not have a law that gives you that right and you cannot file a report about the identity theft, ask to file a "miscellaneous incidents" report instead. Another option is to file a crime report with your state police department.

Some local police departments, as well as many state and federal law enforcement agencies, will let you file an "automated" crime report by phone. Whenever possible, however, file your report in person or at least talk with a human being. It can sometimes be more difficult for a CRA (or an information provider) to confirm the information in an automated identity theft report. As a result, if you want to add an extended alert to your credit histories, you may have to provide the CRA that you contact with additional proof that the theft occurred. Also, automated identity theft reports may make it more difficult for you to resolve issues related to the identity theft with creditors and banks.

🤚 Red Alert!

Don't expect the police to actively look for an identity thief after you've reported the crime to the police. Most police departments don't investigate incidents of identity theft. Don't let that fact discourage you from pressing hard for a crime report.

Report the Crime to the FTC

Whenever you are the victim of identity theft, report that fact to the FTC's ID Theft Hotline by calling 1-877-438-4338 or by going to *www.consumer.gov/idtheft*. The FTC won't help find the identity thief or help you undo the damage to your finances as a result of the theft, but it will share your complaint with identity theft investigators around the country, which could help them find the thief.

OTHER STEPS YOU MAY NEED TO TAKE TO RESOLVE AN IDENTITY THEFT PROBLEM

Depending on how an identity thief has victimized you, you may need to take other actions right away, including the following:

- Contact the Social Security Administration (SSA) immediately if you believe that your Social Security number has been stolen. You can call 1-800-269-0271, report the theft at *www.ssa.gov/oig/hotline/index.htm*, or you can write to: Social Security Administration, Identity Theft Hotline, PO Box 17768, Baltimore, MD 21235-7768. To learn how to obtain a new Social Security number, call the SSA office in your area (the number will be listed in the Blue Pages of your local phone book) or 1-800-772-1213.

- Get in touch with the state motor vehicle department that issued you your driver's license if you think that an identity thief used your name to get a driver's license. Ask that a fraud alert be put on your license and that the department conduct an investigation into the fraud. Once the fraudulent use of your name is confirmed, ask that your license be cancelled and that you be issued a new one.

- Contact the U.S. Postal Inspection Service (USPIS), the law enforcement arm of the U.S. Postal Service, if you think that an identity thief may have stolen your mail or filled out fake change of address forms in order to divert your mail to another mailbox. To locate the USPIS office for your district, look in the Blue Pages of your local phone book or go to *www.usps.gov/websites/depart/inspect*. Also, report the identity theft by completing the form available at *www.usps.com/postalinspectors/mailthft/idtheft.htm* or by writing to: the USPIS, Criminal Investigations Service Center, Attn: Mail Fraud, 222 S. Riverside Plaza, #1250, Chicago, IL 60606.

- Ask your phone service provider to cancel your account and give you a new one if you believe that an identity thief obtained phone service in your name, has been making unauthorized calls from your cell phone, or is having calls billed to one of your phone numbers. Do the same if the identity thief is using your calling card. When you open the new accounts, get new PIN numbers. Also, ask each phone service provider what you must do to get all of the fraudulent phone charges discharged. If you have problems canceling the fraudulent account(s) and/or getting the fraudulent charges discharged, contact:

  - Your state Public Utility Commission for local service. You can find the listing for this office in the Blue Pages of your local phone book.

  - The Federal Communications Commission (FCC) for cellular phones and long distance service. You contact the FCC at 1-888-225-5322 or by writing to the FCC at Consumer Information Bureau, 445 12th Street, S.W., Room 5A863, Washington, DC 20554. You can also file a complaint online at *www.fcc.gov*.

- Contact the U.S. Department of State (USDS) if your passport has been stolen or if you lose it. You can report the theft or loss at the USDS' website, *www.travel.state.gov/passport/passport_1738.html*, or by calling the USDS field office for your area. The contact information will be in your phone book's Blue Pages.

■ Contact your brokerage company, if you believe that an identity thief has accessed your brokerage account, to find out what you can do to protect the account from additional fraud. Also, read your account brokerage agreement about your rights and responsibilities and notify the Securities and Exchange Commission (*www.sec.gov*) and the National Association of Securities Dealers (*www.nasd.org*). Unfortunately, however, if the identity thief has stolen money from your brokerage account or cashed in any of your investments, there is no law that entitles you to get your money back.

■ Get in touch with the IRS immediately if you believe that an identity thief filed a fraudulent federal tax return in your name or committed some other sort of fraud related to your federal taxes. Go to the IRS website (*www.irs.gov*) and type in "identity fraud" for information about what to do, or call the IRS Taxpayer Advocate Service at 1-877-777-4778. Also, because dealing with the IRS can be extremely frustrating, you may want to consult with a tax attorney.

■ Contact the U.S. Department of Education (DOE) hotline if you believe that an identity thief may have obtained a student loan in your name. Request that the student loan account be closed and that you not be held responsible for repaying any of the fraudulent loan amounts. To make this request call the DOE's hotline at 1-800-647-8733, email the hotline at *oig.hotline@ ed.gov*, or download the form at *www.ed.gov/about/offices/list/ oig/hotlineform.html*. You should also contact the financial aid office of the school that the identity thief may be attending.

IF YOU CAN'T RESOLVE AN IDENTITY THEFT PROBLEM ON YOUR OWN

If you have trouble resolving an identity problem, talk with a consumer law attorney who has specific experience helping victims of identity theft. A letter from the attorney may clear up the problem. On the other hand, the attorney may suggest that you file a lawsuit to undo the damage an identity thief has done to your life and to prevent additional damage.

To locate a qualified attorney, contact the National Association of Consumer Advocates at *www.naca.net* or by calling 1-202-452-1989 or your local or state bar association. If your income is low, you may be able to get help from the legal aid office in your area or from the National Foundation for Credit Counseling, *www.nfcc.org* or 1-800-388-2227.

Resources

Check out this list of resources for more information and advice about credit types, credit reporting, credit scores, rebuilding your credit, and identity theft. The list includes websites and books, as well as nonprofit organizations and federal government agencies.

BOOKS

The Bankruptcy Kit (3d ed.) by John Ventura (Kaplan). This book guides you through the bankruptcy process from start to finish.

The Budget Kit: The Common Cents Money Management Workbook (4th ed.) by Judy Lawrence (Kaplan). This budgeting classic has helped countless consumers control and monitor their spending and even helps readers monitor their money in an era of debit cards, online banking, and automatic deposits and drafts. The book is loaded with practical worksheets and forms, and also comes with its own budgeting software.

Frugal Living for Dummies by Deborah Taylor-Hough (Wiley). This book shows you how to spend less and still "live the good life."

Good Advice for a Bad Economy by John Ventura and Mary Reed (Berkeley). Reach for this book when you're hit with an unexpected financial setback — like a job loss or an expensive illness—that is taking a toll on your finances. It is full of compassionate and helpful advice and information about how to get through the crisis with minimal damage to your finances.

It's More Than Money—It's Your Life!: The New Money Club for Women by Candace Bahr and Ginita Wall (Wiley). This fun-to-read book provides women with practical information and advice about the money issues women commonly face, and helps them become smarter money managers.

Live Well on Less Than You Think: The New York Times Guide to Achieving Your Financial Freedom by Fred Brock (Times). The theme of this book is that every time you cut your expenses, you effectively give yourself a pay increase. The book provides practical information and advice on credit, debt, owning a home, buying or leasing a car, insurance, and banking, among other things.

Managing Debt for Dummies by John Ventura and Mary Reed (Wiley). This book tells you everything you need to know when you owe too much to your creditors.

The Money Tracker: Find the Cash to Get What You Really Want by Judy Lawrence (Advisor). This book helps you figure out exactly what you do with your money. It also helps you to understand the spending patterns that undermine your ability to achieve your financial goals and uses success stories and quizzes to help motivate you to develop a healthier relationship with money. A good companion to Lawrence's *The Budget Kit*.

Your Money or Your Life: Transforming Your Relationship with Money and Achieving Financial Independence by Joe Dominguez and Vicki Robin (Penguin). Use this book to help assess and change the role that money plays in your life, with the goal of being able to live on what you earn. This book spawned the voluntary simplicity movement, which is about being aware of your spending and making choices about what you do with your money, rather than using credit to have it all.

WEBSITES

AllThingsFrugal.com This site is loaded with information about how to make every penny count in every area of your life.

Bankrate.com Here, you'll find a wealth of information about all aspects of credit repair, credit reporting, credit scoring, applying for and using credit, and identity theft, as well as a wide variety of online calculators to help you manage your finances.

BetterBudgeting.com This site features an e-zine that's "Dedicated to Helping Families Live a Better Life, Not by Spending More Money, but Less!" as well as a host of helpful budgeting calculators.

CardRatings.com Established by U.S. Citizens for Fair Credit Card Terms, Inc., you can use this site to get detailed information about more than 1,000 different credit cards, including cards for consumers with no credit or poor credit, cards with low introductory rates, cards that offer points or rewards when you use them, and so on. It also features consumer reviews of various credit cards, with new reviews added daily, along with information about credit reports, credit scores, and rebuilding credit, together with sample letters to write when you are trying to resolve credit-related problems.

CardWeb.com Go to this site to search for a credit card that meets your needs. If you're not sure what type of credit card might be best for you, fill out the site's online questionnaire and you'll receive recommendations for specific cards.

DebtAdvice.org The information at this site is provided by various nonprofit credit counseling agencies that are members of the National Foundation for Consumer Credit. You'll find tips for selecting the right credit counseling agency, information about credit and credit reporting, a budgeting calculator, and an online directory for finding an NFCC-affiliated agency near you, or one that offers credit counseling by phone.

DebtSmart.com This site is a great resource for anyone who wants to get smarter about managing debt, using credit cards, and rebuilding credit, among other topics. You can also find out about good deals on credit cards at this site and sign up to have a free DebtSmart newsletter sent directly to your computer twice every month.

Equifax.com Besides being able to purchase your Equifax credit report at this site, it also offers a considerable amount of good, solid information on all aspects of the Fair Credit Reporting Act, as well as advice for how to cope financially with life events like losing your job, getting married or divorced, or being widowed. There is also an area that helps you to prepare to buy a home and a car by walking you through all of the issues to consider before making your purchases.

Experian.com You'll find pretty much the same information here as you can find at the Equifax site, although the information at this site is not always as complete.

Thefrugallife.com This site offers ideas for "living well with what you have."

myFICO.com In addition to ordering your FICO scores at this site, you can also learn about credit scoring and identity theft by reading its downloadable publications. You can also use online calculators to figure out whether you should consolidate your credit card debts, refinance your home, and to determine which loan is better, among other things.

RealFreebies.com Use this site to find out about offers for free items, including free food samples, body care products, cleaning supplies, and more.

StopDebtCollectorsCold.com Go to this site if you're having problems with debt collectors or if you just want to become more informed about your federal debt collection rights.

TransUnion.com This CRA's website offers some resources the two others don't, including online worksheets for building a budget, improving your credit, reducing your debts, and fighting identity theft. It also offers an easy-to-use step-by-step guide to improving your finances, among other things.

WIFE.org WIFE stands for Women's Institute for Financial Education. This site is dedicated to helping women become financially independent. Guys, you'll learn something here too!

NONPROFIT ORGANIZATIONS AND FEDERAL AGENCIES

Debtors Anonymous This national organization uses the proven techniques of Alcoholics Anonymous to help consumers overcome their spending problems. There are Debtors Anonymous chapters around the country. Visit *www.debtorsanonymous.org* or call 1-781-453-2743 to contact.

Federal Trade Commission (FTC) This federal regulatory agency is responsible for enforcing a wide array of consumer laws, including the *Fair Credit Reporting Act*, the *Fair Debt Collection Practices Act*, and the *Credit Repair Organizations Act*. It also publishes numerous publications on all aspects of credit reporting and credit scoring, credit cards, debt collectors, identity theft, and consumers laws, among other subjects. Visit *www.ftc.gov or* call 1-877-382-4357 to contact.

National Consumer Law Center A national advocate for low-income consumers helps them make consumer laws work for them. Visit *www.consumerlaw.org or* call 1-617-542-8010 to contact.

Index

A

Account information, 36-37, 45
    identity theft and, 199
    missing, 94-96
Accreditation, 114
Address change, 183
Adjusted balance, 134
Adverse action, 12, 23, 30
AICCCA. See Association of Independent Consumer Credit Counseling Agencies
American Express, 6, 131, 148
American Mental Health Counselor's Association (AMHCA), 129
Amount owed, 66
Annual percentage rate (APR), 133, 134
AnnualCreditReport.com, 27
APR. See Annual percentage rate
Arrests, 11, 39
Association of Independent Consumer Credit Counseling Agencies (AICCCA), 111
ATM cards, 200-201
Attorney.com, 157
Attorney-locate web site, 157-58
Attorneys general, 13, 114
Authorized user, 106-7
Automatic stay, 175
Automobile insurance claims, 19
Average daily balance, 134

B

Background
    check report, 23
    screening companies, 20-22
Balance calculation method, 134
Banana Republic, 131
Bank accounts, 200-201

Banking commission, 114
Bank loan, 96-98
Bankrate.com, 94, 100
Bankruptcies, 11, 175-77
Bankruptcy attorney, 90, 176
Bar associations, 157
Better Business Bureau (BBB), 114
Book resources, 209-10
Brokerage company, 207
Budget, 80-82, 137
    building, 82-88
    monitoring, 85-86
    review, 138, 170
    sample monthly household, 87-88
Businesses, 9
Business opportunity promoters, 164-65

C

Capacity, 136
Car
    loan, 67, 138
    repossessed, 38
CardWeb.com, 100
CCRRA. See Consumer Credit Reporting Reform Act
Certegy, 19
Certificate of deposit (CD), 94, 99
Certified mail, 155
Chapter 7, 175, 176-77
Chapter 13, 11, 175, 176
Character, 136
Charge offs, 78-79
Check-reporting companies/registries, 18-19
CheckRite, 19
Check writing, 178, 200-201
Chevron, 102
ChexSystems, 19
Child support, 9, 39, 170
ChoicePoint, 19, 20, 22
Civil lawsuits, 11
Classified ads, 167
Closing accounts, 66
CLUE Reports, 19
Collateral, 98, 132, 136, 172
Collection agencies, 9
    accounts, 46

notification, 31
Comparison shopping, 138
Complaint letter, 15
Concessions, 171
Consumer Credit File Rights under State and Federal Law, 118
Consumer Credit Reporting Reform Act (CCRRA), 7, 11, 24
Consumer Data Information Association, 4
Consumer law attorney, 56, 57, 95, 157-59, 208
Consumer laws, 142-54
Consumer protection office, 114
Consumer rights, 138, 154-60
Contingent fee basis, 16, 23, 158
Contracts, 120
Cooling-off period, 119
Cosigning, 105,137, 172
Court order, 9
Craigslist.org, 166
CRAs. See Credit reporting agencies
Credit account
    applied for, 66
    balances, 68
    billing statement dispute, 146-48
    closings, 45
    openings, 66, 200
    payment history, 65
    reporting, 94-96
Credit bureau, 24
Credit card
    balances, 137-38
    offers, to avoid, 102-4
    scams, 104
Credit counseling agencies, 81, 110-14, 117, 172, 178
Credit criteria, 136
Credit file, 4, 23, 183
Credit fix-it organizations, 75
Credit history, 4
    damaged, 89-90
    fee for, 26-29
    impact of negative information, 10-11
    information in, 5-6
    longevity, 66
    ordering, 25-26
    organization of, 39-40
    in own name, 141
    rebuilding, vi, vii. See also Credit rebuilding

review of, 138
revision, 13
who can view, 7-10
Credit mix, 67
Credit monitoring, 41-42, 187
Creditors, 7, 10
    agreements with, 172
    contacting, 168-72
Credit Practices Rule, 149-50
Credit protection, 125
Credit rebuilding
    adding positive information, 94-96
    authorized user, 106-7
    bank loan, 96-98
    budgeting, 80-82
    card offers to avoid, 102-4
    charge offs, 78-79
    cosigners, 105
    credible help, 109-14
    facing facts, 89-90
    gasoline cards, 102
    managing negative information, 74-80
    preliminary steps, 73-74
    retail charge cards, 102
    secured Visa, MasterCard, 98-101
    setting up a budget, 82-88
    tax problems, 79-80
    when to start, 93-94
    written statement, 75-77
Credit record, 4, 23
    common errors in, 45-46
    corrections, 43-44, 53-54
    disputes, 201-2
    reviewing, 44-45
Credit repair. See also Credit rebuilding
    rip-off, 115-17
    scam victim recourse, 121
Credit Repair Organizations Act (CROA), 118-20, 138, 142
Credit report, 4, 23
    free copy, 12-13
    information overview, 36-39
    ordering, 32-35
    paying for, 31-32
Credit reporting, v, vi
    rights, v, 11-16

Credit reporting agencies (CRAs), 4-5, 25
    background on, 4
    credit scores by, 61-62
    initiating investigation with, 48-53
    investigation process, 47
    negative information challenging, 116
    other products of, 40-42
    rights, 12-13
    sources for information in, 6-7
Credit score, v, 4, 14, 23, 59-60
Credit shopping, 133-35
Credit types, 131-32
Credit use, 177
Crime reporting, 202-4
CROA. See Credit Repair Organizations Act

D

D.A. See Debtors Anonymous
Damage control, 161-62
    acknowledgment of problem, 162
    actions never to take, 177-79
    avoiding scams, 164-65
    contacting creditors, 168-72
    debt consolidation, 173-75
    increasing income, 163-64
    selling belongings, 166-67
    spending less, 162-63
Damages, 159
Debit cards, 200-201
Debt
    analysis, 168-70
    consolidation, 173-73
    payments, 177
    repayment, 137
    too much, 139-41
Debt collectors, 150-53, 202
Debtors Anonymous (D.A.), 89, 130
Default clause, 23, 133
Deficit, 85
Department of Banking, 114
Direct Marketing Association (DMA), 191-92, 193
Discover Card, 6, 148
Disney World, 3
Dispute form, 48
Divorce, 90, 138, 141

DMA. See Direct Marketing Association, 191-92
Doctor, 129
Driver's license, 205
Dumpster diving, 182
Duty alerts, 199

E

eBay trading assistant, 166
ECOA. See Equal Credit Opportunity Act
Educated score, 62
EFTA. See Electronic Fund Transfer Act
EIN. See Employer Identification Number
Electronic Fund Transfer Act (EFTA), 153-54, 200
Emergency fund, 81
Employee background check, 20
Employer, 8, 13
Employer Identification Number (EIN), 116
Equal Credit Opportunity Act (ECOA), 143-45
Equifax, v, 4, 12, 22, 23, 25, 27
    Classic FICO score, 64
    credit rebuilding, 74
    credit report preview, 39
    credit scores, 62-63
    dispute form, 48
    fraud alerts, 198
    ordering credit report online, 33
Erroneous information, 55-56
Estimated score, 62
Expansion score, 64
Expenses, 83-84, 85
Experian, v, 4, 12, 22, 23, 25, 27
    credit rebuilding, 74
    credit report preview, 39
    credit scores, 62
    dispute form, 49
    fraud alerts, 198
    ordering credit report online, 33
Exxon, 102

F

FACTA. See Fair and Accurate Credit Transactions Act
Fair and Accurate Credit Transactions Act (FACTA), 24
    arrests, 12
    credit history access, 7
    credit history fees, 26

identity theft and, 185, 197
investigations under, 57
rights under, 11, 142
Fair Credit Billing Act (FCBA), 145-49, 199
Fair Credit Reporting Act (FCRA), 24
adverse actions, 30
background check, 20-22, 23
bankruptcy and, 176
credit history access, 7
disputing inaccurate information, 42,44
expedited investigations, 52-53
fraud alert, 30
free credit reports, 26, 30-31
missing information, 95
negative information, 68, 74, 76
other national consumer reporting agencies governed by, 17-22
rip-offs, 115
rights under, 11-12, 138
Fair Debt Collection Practices Act (FDCPA), 150-53
Fair Isaac Corporation, 60, 63-64, 67
False claims, 119
Family, 129, 157
FCBA. See Fair Credit Billing Act
FCRA. See Fair Credit Reporting Act
FDCPA. See Fair Debt Collection Practices Act
Federal agencies, 213
Federal Communications Commission (FCC), 206
Federal Deposit Insurance Corporation, 156
Federal Reserve Board, 156
Federal taxes, past due, 170
Federal Trade Commission (FTC), 24, 15-16, 156, 157
complaint filing, 56
Credit Practices Rule, 149-50
Identity theft, 181-82, 185, 191, 192
ID Theft Affidavit, 195
900 numbers, 104
scams, 28, 121
Theft Hotline, 205
Fees, 135
FICO credit scores, 59
FICO score, vi, vii, 136, 138, 161
classic, 63-64
credit reports and, 41, 45, 59
factors determining, 65-67
learning, 64-65

raising, 67-69
File segregation, 115
Financial goals, 81
Financial involvement, 141
Financial Modernization and Privacy Act, 192-93
Financial ratios, 138
Financial Services Modernization Act (FSMA), 192-93
Fixed percentage rate, 133-34
Foreclosure, 38
401(k) plan loan, 174
Fraud alert, 30, 194, 197-99
Fraudulent charges, 194
FreeCreditReport.com, 27
Friends, 129, 157
FSMA. See Financial Services Modernization Act
FTC. See Federal Trade Commission

G

Garage sales, 167
Garnished paycheck, 170
Gasoline cards, 102, 103
Goal setting, 82-83, 137
Government agencies, 9, 155-57
Grace period, 134-35

H

Happiness, 127
Home Depot, 131
Home equity loan, 138, 175
Homeowners' insurance claims, 19
Household budget, 74

I

ID Theft Affidavit, 195
Identifying information, 36, 45
Identity theft, vi, 115, 181-82
    federal laws, 12, 17, 185
    FICO scores and, 65, 67
    free credit reports, 30
    how happens, 182-84
    insurance, 190
    other steps to take, 205-8
    protecting from, 187-93
    report, 199
    signs of, 193-94

websites and, 28
what happens, 186-87
when it's stolen, 194-205
Identity Theft and Assumption Deterrence Act (ITADA), 185
ID Theft Affidavit, 195
Income sources, 84-85
Incomplete information, 46
Individuals, 9
Information
    correcting inaccurate, v
    identifying, 5
    negative, 10-11
Inquiries, 5, 37-38
Instant gratification, 127
Insurance companies, 7-8, 9
Intermediate-term goals, 82
Investigation
    corrected information, 53-55
    information provider, 57
    initiation, 48-53
    problems with, 57-59
    process, 47
    record contains no error, 55-56
    reports, 21-22, 24
Investors, 9
IRS installment plan, 79-80
IRS Taxpayer Advocate Service, 207
ISO Insurance Services, 19
ITADA. See Identity Theft and Assumption Deterrence Act

J

Javelin Strategy & Research, 182
Job application, 30-31
Job skills, 141
Joint credit, 141
Judgments, 11, 38

L

Landlords, 8
Lawsuit, 14
    filing, 16-17
    planning, 159-60
Lawyers.com, 157
Legal judgment, 24
Legitimate business need, 10

Letter, viii
    account billing statement dispute, 146-48
    disputing fraudulent charges, 199-200
    free credit report, 29
    investigation request, 49-51
    ordering credit report, 35
    ordering free credit report, 29
    written credit statement, 75-77
Lien, 132
Life coach, 130
Life insurance loan, 174
Loan officers, 96-98
Loan servicers, 9
Long-term goals, 83
Los Angeles Electronic Crimes Task Force, 28

M

Mail fraud, 206
Martindale.com, 157
MasterCard
    credit mix and, 67
    credit practices, 149
    fair billing, 145, 148
    identity theft and, 201
    information from 6, 7
    number of, 102
    payment history, 95
    qualifying for, 82
    secured, 98-101
    unsecured, 131
Medical Information Bureau (MIB), 6, 18
Mental Health America (MHA), 129
Mental health association, 129
Mental health professionals, 129-30
MIB. See Medical Information Bureau
Money, 126-28
Money judgments, 5, 38
Money management
    basics, 130-36
    changing role of, 129-30
    mind-sets and, 127-28
    rules of thumb, 137-38
    skills, 89
Mortgage, 67, 95, 138
Motor vehicle department, 205

N

National Association of Attorneys General, 13, 114
National Association of Consumer Advocates, 157, 208
National Association of Securities Dealers, 207
National Consumer Law Center, 157
National consumer specialty reporting agencies, 24
National credit reporting agency, 24
National Credit Union Administration, 156
National Foundation for Credit Counseling (NFCC), 110-11, 208
Negative information, 46
Negligently noncompliant, 17
NextGen score, 64
NFCC. See National Foundation for Credit Counseling
900 number, 102-4, 117
Nonprofit organizations, 213
Nonrevolving credit, 131
Notification, 12, 13

O

Offer in compromise, 80
Office of the Comptroller of the Currency, 156
Office of Thrift Supervision, 156
OnGuardOnline.gov, 189
Opt-out number, 38
Opt-out offers, 191-93

P

Paid as agreed, 78
Paid charge off, 78
Paper trail, 196-97
Passport, 206
Past-due rent, 170
Performance bond, 113
Periodic interest rate, 134
Personal finance, vi, vii
Personal identification number (PIN), 181
Personal representative, 199
Phishing, 183
Phone conversations log, 59
Phone service provider, 206
Police report, 195
Pre-approved offers, 14-15, 24, 38, 100
Predatory lenders, 175
Prescreened offers, 14-15, 24

Promises, 178
Property taxes, 80
Public record information, 5, 6-7, 38-39
Public Utility Commission, 206
Public welfare assistance, 31
Pyramiding, 150

Q-R

Quicken Basic/Deluxe, 83
Record keeping, 196-97
Refinancing, 174
Rental agents, 8
Rental history companies, 19-20
Repossession, 177
Resources, viii
Retail charge cards, 102, 103, 145
Retirement age, 143
Revolving closed-end credit, 131
Revolving open-end credit, 131

S

SafeRent, 20
Savings account, 74, 84, 89, 94, 99, 137
Scams, 164-65
SCAN. See Shared Check Authorization Network
Secret Service, 28
Secured debt, 97-98, 174, 178
Securities and Exchange Commission, 207
Shared Check Authorization Network (SCAN), 19
Short-term goals, 82
Skimming, 183
Skin shedding, 115
Small claims court, 159
Social Security, 32, 116, 188
Social Security Administration (SSA), 205
Social Security Earnings and Benefits Estimate Statement, 189
Social Security number, 5, 45
Spending, 89, 91, 126-28
Spiritual advisor, 130
Spousal debts, 46
SSA. See Social Security Administration
State laws, 13, 31
Store credit cards, 69
Student loan, 171, 207
Subpoena, 9

T

Tax lien, 11, 24, 38, 79-80
TeleCheck, 19
Telemarketing, 191
Tenant Data Services, 20
Theft, 184
Three-in-one reports, 40-41
Timely payments, 67-68
Toll-free dispute line, 51-52
TransUnion, v, 4, 24
    credit history, 25, 27
    credit rebuilding, 74
    credit reports, 22
    credit report preview, 40
    credit scores, 62
    dispute form, 49
    free report from, 12
    fraud alerts, 198
    ordering credit report online, 33
Truth in Lending Act, 133, 142
Two-cycle average balance, 134

U

U.S. Department of Education, 207
U.S. Department of State, 206
U.S. Postal Inspection Service (USPIS), 206
Uncollectible accounts, 6
Universal default clause, 133, 135
Unsecured credit/debt, 98, 131-32, 171, 174, 178
Utilities, 9, 170

V

VantageScore, 63
Variable percentage rate, 133-34
Visa, 131
    credit mix and, 67
    credit practices, 149
    fair billing, 148
    identity theft and, 201
    information from 6, 7
    number of, 102
    payment history, 95
    qualifying for, 82
    secured, 98-101

W-Y

Website resources, 211-13
Willfully noncompliant, 16-17
Written permission, 10
Yard Sale Queen, 167

About the Author

John Ventura is a best selling author, a nationally-board certified bankruptcy attorney and a consumer advocate. He is also an adjunct professor at the University of Houston Law School and director of the Texas Consumer Complaint Center at the Law School, where he supervises law students as they help consumers with their legal problems. John also speaks at law conferences around the country

As a young boy, John dreamed of becoming a Catholic priest so he could help people. In fact, he spent his high school years in a Catholic seminary. After graduating however, John decided to achieve his dream by combining journalism with the law. He envisioned providing ordinary people with affordable, caring legal services and educating them about how to use the law to protect their rights and to avoid legal trouble. In order to achieve his goal therefore, John earned an undergraduate degree in journalism and a law degree from the University of Houston. Later, he and a partner established a law firm in Texas, building it into one of the most successful consumer bankruptcy firms in the state. When that partnership ended, he began a consumer law firm in the Rio Grande Valley of South Texas.

John is the author of 13 books including *The Bankruptcy Kit, 3rd edition*, *The Credit Repair Kit, 4th edition*, *Managing Debt for Dummies*, *Law for Dummies, 2nd edition*, *Divorce for Dummies, 2nd edition*, *Good Advice for a Bad Economy* and the e-book, *Stop Debt Collectors Cold.com*. He has been interviewed about consumer and debt by numerous national media including CNN, NBC, NPR, Bloomberg Television and Radio, The Wall Street Journal, USA Today, Newsweek, Kiplinger's Personal Finance, Money, Inc. Martha Stewart's Living, Bottomline, Entrepreneur, Bankrate.com, CBSMarketWatch.com, and MSNMoney.com, among others. He has also been a frequent guest on local radio programs around the country.

KAPLAN